DEVO
FOR THE
REST OF US

THE NEXT 40 DAYS ON YOUR
JOURNEY OF FAITH

VINCE ANTONUCCI

Tyndale House Publishers, Inc.
Carol Stream, Illinois

Visit Tyndale online at www.tyndale.com.

Visit Vince Antonucci online at http://vinceantonucci.com and http://therestofusresources.com/book.

TYNDALE and Tyndale's quill logo are registered trademarks of Tyndale House Publishers, Inc.

Devo for the Rest of Us: The Next 40 Days on Your Journey of Faith

Designed by Ron Kaufmann

Edited by Jane Vogel

Published in association with the literary agency of the Gates Group, 1403 Walnut Lane, Louisville, Kentucky 40223.

Unless otherwise indicated, all Scripture quotations are taken from the *Holy Bible*, New Living Translation, copyright © 1996, 2004, 2015 by Tyndale House Foundation. Used by permission of Tyndale House Publishers, Inc., Carol Stream, Illinois 60188. All rights reserved.

Scripture quotations marked NIV are taken from the Holy Bible, *New International Version,*® *NIV.*® Copyright © 1973, 1978, 1984, 2011 by Biblica, Inc.® (Some quotations may be from the earlier NIV edition, copyright © 1984.) Used by permission. All rights reserved worldwide.

Scripture quotations marked ESV are taken from *The Holy Bible*, English Standard Version® (ESV®), copyright © 2001 by Crossway, a publishing ministry of Good News Publishers. Used by permission. All rights reserved.

The illustration of the baby in the womb told in Week Four, Day 1, was originally told in *I Became a Christian and All I Got Was This Lousy T-Shirt* (Grand Rapids, MI: Baker, 2008). Adapted and used by permission of Baker Books, a division of Baker Publishing Group.

ISBN 978-1-4964-1095-5

Printed in the United States of America

21   20   19   18   17   16   15
 7   6   5   4   3   2   1

CONTENTS

INTRODUCTION

She sold the tickets. I tore the tickets in half. It was a match made in movie-theater heaven.

My wife and I met while wearing polyester as coworkers in college. We were in charge of letting people enter the theater. And in that theater we began a journey together. We quickly became friends. (She was probably immediately attracted to me. My animal magnetism does that to the ladies. Or . . . it may have been the constant smell of hot, buttered popcorn.) Later we started to date, and we've now been married for more than twenty years. I love her more now than I ever have. (Though I don't know if she's as attracted to me as she used to be. The only animalistic trait I still have is the shape of a potbellied pig.)

How does that happen? How do you start and grow a relationship? Looking back, I realize there have been two critical factors:

Knowledge: You need to get to know a person to grow the relationship. And the more you know, the deeper the relationship goes.

Habits: At the beginning of a relationship, there's a newness that generates excitement. As the relationship continues, it's easy to get distracted and grow apart. My wife and I have routines that keep us connected. We go out on a date every week. We talk each night after work. We text each other to check in once or twice a day. We get out of town for a weekend away once or twice a year.

Thinking about it, I realize that increasing knowledge and repeating habits are the two critical factors in *all* my relationships. It looks a bit different, but these factors are how I've grown my relationships with my kids, friends, and coworkers.

And the same is true with God.

What God is looking to have with us is a relationship, not a religion. Although it may look a bit different, the way you grow a relationship with God is the same way you grow a relationship with anyone else.

Knowledge: You need to get to know God. The more you know God, the deeper the relationship can go.

Habits: At the beginning of a relationship with God, there's a newness that generates excitement. But there are *so many* factors that work to distract people from God and pull them away from him. In the classic devotional book *My Utmost for His Highest*, Oswald Chambers writes, "Routine is God's way of saving us between our times of inspiration."

This book is designed to increase your knowledge of God and help you establish habits that will keep you connected and growing in your love for him for the rest of your life.

If you're new to faith or coming back to God after some time away, this book will be a perfect fit for your spiritual needs. If your faith is more established, this book will be a challenging refresher that will deepen your love for God and your commitment to living the life he has for you.

The book is divided into forty days. Each day there's a short reading, a passage to look up in the Bible, something to pray about, and an assignment. The assignment might be something for you to think about or to try doing that day. Why divide this book up into forty days? Because we're establishing habits! My hope is that those habits will stay with you for a lifetime.

There are two ways you can use this book:

- You can read it on your own. That will work!

- You can use it in a group. In the back of the book are group-discussion questions. The people in your group can each do five readings a week and then talk through the discussion questions for that section at your weekly get-together.

However you use it, this book can help you as you start or continue on your journey.

As I move forward and stumble through my journey, I know I need hope, so I try to keep the end in mind; I think a lot about heaven. I have questions about heaven.

Will we receive a ticket and have it ripped in half to enter heaven? I don't know. (But if so, I am convinced the guy who does it will be wearing polyester.)

Will it smell like hot, buttered popcorn in heaven? I don't know. (But if so, I will *not* complain.)

One thing I feel sure of is that in heaven, the presence of God will be so real he will be impossible to ignore, and his love will be so tangible we won't be distracted by lesser things.

Until then, we will continue to struggle. Jesus promised that in this world we will have trouble.* It won't be easy. We need all the help we can get. I pray this book will be a big help to you in growing your relationship with God as you journey with him toward heaven.

---

* See John 16:33.

Hungry

*We sense that something is missing. We're
lacking something we know we need.*

But many of us struggle to name that longing.

*What if what we're hungry for is God
and what only God can give us?*

And what if we can have it if we just turn to him?

Day 1

LONGING FOR LOVE

*Jesus replied, "I am the bread of life. Whoever comes
to me will never be hungry again."*

JOHN 6:35

"DADDEEEE, I'M HUNGEEEE."

Silence.

"Daddeeee, I'm hungeeee."

My then three-year-old son was entirely cute and a little annoying.* About twenty times a day he would call out from wherever he was in the house.

"Daddeeee, I'm hungeeee."

"Dawson, you're fine," I would respond. "You ate just a little bit ago. We'll be eating soon. You're fine."

Silence.

"No, Daddeeee. I'm weally hungeeee. I'm starving, Daddeeee."

My son was a bit melodramatic. But, on the other hand, maybe he was on to something.

---

* Am I allowed to say my son was annoying?

In fact, what I think he was on to is the human condition. We're hungry. We're all hungry. And I believe what we're hungry for is love. *Perfect* love.

Ted

Ted sat at the production meeting before our service. Before we talk through the elements of our service, we always recognize and cheer for any new volunteer. That day, Ted was doing a "first serve" running the sound board. He was an ex-hippie from San Francisco who used to run sound for the Grateful Dead.

We cheered for Ted. (Normal.)

He blushed. (Normal.)

He gave a little speech. (Not normal.)

"Thank you," he said. "I started coming a few weeks ago because my sister in Texas insisted I try this church. I'm not a church person, and didn't think I'd like it at all, but I did. I just want to be up front with you guys. I don't believe any of the stuff you believe. But I'm hoping maybe your faith rubs off on me."

I asked him why, if he didn't believe, he kept coming back.

"Well, I . . ." Ted paused. "I've never felt as loved as I do here."

Wookin' Pa Nub

Back in the eighties, Eddie Murphy used to do an impression of Buckwheat from the Little Rascals. If you remember the Little Rascals, you know Buckwheat never mastered the ability to pronounce certain words. One Eddie Murphy skit was a commercial for a fake "Buckwheat Sings" album featuring the hit "Wookin' pa nub in all da wong paces. Wookin' pa nub."

That's exactly the problem. People are looking for love, but in all the wrong places.

We long for love. A deeper love than we receive from other people. We long for a love that is truly unconditional and utterly dependable. A love that draws us in and drives out our fear. A love that is pure enough to fit well in our hearts and big enough to fill the gaping hole we find in them. We yearn for perfect love.

And so we look. As children we look to our parents, later we look for our love need to be met in romantic relationships, and still later in our kids. Some of us try to substitute success or food or money or drugs or fame for love, but no matter how much we get, we still find ourselves longing.

The love we're looking for is too perfect for anything in this world to be able to satisfy us.

It's a love that only God can give us.

And he wants to. The Bible says God wants to lavish it on us* and pour it into our hearts.** And God's love is big enough to meet our love need. In fact, it's bigger than we can even understand.

> I pray that you, being rooted and established in love, may
> have power, together with all the Lord's holy people, to
> grasp how wide and long and high and deep is the love of
> Christ, and to know this love that surpasses knowledge—
> that you may be filled to the measure of all the fullness
> of God.***

I Finally Found What I've Been Looking For

Two weekends ago I preached a sermon challenging people to bet their lives on Jesus. (I'm in Vegas; people here understand gambling metaphors.) "We all bet our lives on something," I said. "We seek our identity and meaning from something. We pour our lives into something. We're trusting something with our lives and for our eternity. Make Jesus your something. Bet your life on Jesus."

I led people who wanted to make Jesus their Savior and Lord in

---

* See 1 John 3:1, NIV.
** See Romans 5:5, NIV.
*** Ephesians 3:17-19, NIV.

5

a prayer, then told them to sign up for the baptisms that would be happening the following week.

After the service Ted walked up and said, "Where do I sign up? I'm all in."

It had been about four months since his first visit. Since then he had been reading the Bible every day. He dove into serving. He made some friends. One of our pastors shared the gospel with him over coffee. But mostly, he had felt loved, and he had learned about and experienced the love of God. And that's what he had been wookin' pa his entire life.

Last weekend Ted stood in front of a room full of people and shared his story. (He took fourteen minutes!) Ted said his whole life he'd had no interest in God because he had assumed God had no interest in him. But he had always longed for something he could never find. At our church he had found it. He said, "I just can't believe God loves me. I can't believe God wants a guy like me. I have something to wake up for every day now. I wake up with a smile. I can't wait to read my Bible. The reading plan will say to read like James 1. But it's so good I'll just keep reading, like all the way to James 12. Well, I don't know if there really is a James 12." (There is no James 12. Ted will figure that out soon.)

He said, again, and again, and again, "I just can't believe God loves me. I can't believe God would want a guy like me. I finally found what I've been looking for."

Call to Him

We're hungeeeee. And God is what we're hungry for.

When my son would call, "Daddeeee, I'm hungeeee," and I knew he really *was* hungry, you know what I would do? I would get him something to eat. Of course I would. How can you say no when your kid calls out to you like that?

You are God's kid.

When you look up to him with big eyes and say, "Daddy, I'm hungry," his heart melts.

And he will always respond to that cry.

•   •   •

Now What?

➤ Read Jeremiah 29:12-13.

➤ What would it look like for you to seek God with all your heart?

➤ Prayer is talking to God. Some people make it more complicated, and it intimidates them into not praying at all. But prayer is just talking to God. God invites us to talk to him from our hearts, to talk to him about anything and everything, and to feel free to speak casually to him. Prayer is a big part of how we grow in our relationship with him. Each day you'll be given something to pray about. Hopefully, it will lead you each day into spending more time talking to God about other things, and over the forty days, into the habit of praying every day. Today, ask God to help you to be consistent doing all forty days of this book and for it to establish lifelong habits that will keep you connected to him.

Day 2

RUNNING ON EMPTY

God . . . has planted eternity in the human heart.

ECCLESIASTES 3:11

YOU ARE MORE THAN A PHYSICAL BODY. You know that.

Whatever it is that you are, you are on a journey. You know that.

Everything that moves needs fuel. Cars need gas. Bodies need food. So what fuel do we need for our life's journey?

Is it possible you're running on *bad gas*?

One time my car was idling kind of rough. Someone asked me, "Did you get gas at . . ." and named a local gas station.

"Yeah," I answered. "Why?"

She told me, "They have bad gas. They're known for watering down their gas."

I wonder if you're running on bad fuel. What is it that moves and restores and sustains you? Is it your job? Money? Success? Sex? The approval of other people? Living up to your parents' expectations? Drugs? Feeling significant? Looking good?

If so, how's that working for you?

My guess is that you find it unfulfilling, and your life has been kind of rough.

And running on bad fuel may leave you with *no gas*.

Have you ever run out of gas with your car? When it happens you feel so stupid, but it's just that you weren't thinking about it. You weren't paying attention to the fuel gauge. Your focus was on something else.

One Christmas Day our church did a banquet for homeless people. It was awesome. Somehow the news media heard about it, and a reporter showed up and told me there would be a story about it in the paper the next day. The next morning my car was low on gas, so I drove to a gas station, pulled up, put the nozzle in, and walked away as it was filling up. I went into the little store and bought the newspaper. As I walked back to my car I found the article and started reading. I got into my car, started it, pulled away, and heard a sound. It was a loud thud, followed by a metallic scraping noise. I looked back and realized I hadn't taken the nozzle out of my car. As I drove away, the nozzle and hose ripped out of the gas pump, and I was dragging them behind my car. Wow.

Many of us are so focused on other things (success, appearance, money, romance) that we don't pay attention to how we're doing inside, until one day we realize we're empty. Then we figure it's because we haven't filled our lives with enough of the things we're seeking in this world, so we pursue more. Hopefully it won't take our entire lives to understand that no amount of success or romance will fill our emptiness.

Several years ago Tom Brady was interviewed on *60 Minutes*. Tom Brady is perhaps the most successful current athlete in America, having now won the Super Bowl four times. He's good looking. He's rich, living in a twenty-million dollar mansion in California. He's married to Gisele Bündchen, a Victoria's Secret supermodel. If externals can fill a person up, Tom Brady should be overflowing.[*] In

---

[*] Okay—he did get caught up in Deflategate and suspended, but that was years later. At the time of this interview, it seemed like he had everything.

the interview he said, "Why do I have three Super Bowl rings and still think there's something greater out there for me? I mean, maybe a lot of people would say, 'Hey man, this is what is.' I reached my goal, my dream, my life. I think, 'God, it's got to be more than this.' I mean this isn't, this can't be what it's all cracked up to be. . . . I love playing football and I love being quarterback for this team. But at the same time, I think there are a lot of other parts about me that I'm trying to find." Tom Brady seems to have it all, but he feels like it's not enough. He may not know it, but he's running on empty.

We may be running on bad gas, we may be running on empty, and at some point we may get detached from an ability to refuel at all. Maybe you've been there. Maybe you *are* there. Struggling to find a reason to get out of bed in the morning. Wondering what it's all about. Feeling no hope for a better future. I think some people, as they continue on in their life's journey, go from having bad gas, to no gas, to an inability to refuel at all. It's like they have no lust left for life. They don't care anymore.

Why is it that we sense this emptiness and feel unfilled?

The Bible says that "God . . . has planted eternity in the human heart."* God has made us for something bigger and better than this world. He put eternity in our hearts.

It's what sets humans apart.

I have a dog. My dog lies around all day. Occasionally he plays with a ball. My dog is very content lying around all day and occasionally playing with a ball. He never asks himself, *Why am I lying around all day and occasionally playing with a ball?* He never thinks, *I'm kind of disappointed in myself. I'm not really growing much as a Pomeranian. I think I need to figure out what I'm missing. Why do I exist? Is this really all there is?*

That will never happen, because God didn't plant eternity in my dog's heart.

---

* Ecclesiastes 3:11.

But he did in mine. And he did in yours. He put eternity in our hearts.

That's our curse. It's why we can't be satisfied with the things this world offers.

It's also one of God's greatest *blessings*. Because we won't be satisfied with the things this world offers. God put that craving in our hearts so we would crave him. Because he knows he's the only thing that can fill us.

Jesus says, "I have come that they may have life, and have it to the full."* Jesus came so you can be full. The Bible says, "May the God of hope fill you with all joy and peace as you trust in him, so that you may overflow."**

You don't have to run on empty.

You can be full. Filled to overflowing.

But only if you realize that what you're hungry for is God, if you turn to him, and if he becomes the fuel you run on.

• • •

Now What?

> Read Ephesians 3:14-21.

> That passage talks about having Jesus live in our hearts, being established in God's love, and being filled with God. If you had to add one new habit to your life that you think would help all that to become a reality for you, what would it be? And . . . when will you add it?

> Ask God to show you signs that you've been running on empty and how he can fill you up.

* John 10:10, NIV.
** Romans 15:13, NIV.

Day 3

DESPERATE FOR FORGIVENESS

If we confess our sins to him, he is faithful and just

to forgive us our sins.

1 John 1:9

Have you ever been guilty? Not just *felt* guilty but actually *been* guilty?

In 2009 I moved from Virginia Beach, Virginia, to Las Vegas to start a new church. You may know that. Here's something you may not know: when I moved to Nevada, I was wanted by the police in Virginia.

About a week before heading west, we went to visit some friends. We left our dog with a family in Virginia Beach. I was supposed to get back to pick up our dog on Sunday night around nine o'clock, but I was running late. Really late. And I felt really bad. The family had young kids. They were waiting up for me to arrive. So I was driving fast. Really fast.

I was praying, *God, I know I'm speeding. But I'm doing it to be nice to this family. Please don't let me get pulled over!* when I saw the flashing lights behind me and heard the siren. Sometimes God doesn't answer our prayers. Sometimes God *shouldn't* answer our prayers.

The police officer asked, "Do you know how fast you were going?"

I told him, "It's because of my dog. This family . . . I'm speeding to be nice."

He said, "You were going ninety-two in a fifty-five." In my defense, I thought I was going ninety-two in a sixty-five. But . . . I was guilty.

He gave me a ticket and informed me I had to be in court on February 20.

"I can't be in court in February," I told him. "I'm moving to Las Vegas next week. Can I just plead guilty and pay my fine through the mail?"

"This isn't a traffic ticket." He sounded angry. "You were going more than thirty miles per hour over the speed limit, so this is a Class 1 misdemeanor. That's a *criminal* charge. You *have to* show up in court for a criminal charge."

"I really can't." I sounded pathetic. "I can't afford to fly back just for a trial."

"If you don't show up," he said very sternly, "there will be a warrant out for your arrest. You will be wanted in the state of Virginia."

The next week I moved to Las Vegas. And . . . I didn't go back for my trial. And there *was* a warrant out for my arrest in Virginia.

I was guilty. And I needed help.

Fortunately, I had a friend in Virginia who was a lawyer.

I called on him, and he was able to take care of my problem for me.

Las Vegas

I didn't plan on having a warrant out for my arrest when I moved to start a church in Las Vegas, but I hoped it might give me some street cred.

And, as it turned out, one of the first people I met and became friends with was a guy who had just gotten out of prison. Shortly after meeting, we sat at a breakfast restaurant. He was crying. He believed in God, and he wanted to believe that God believed in him. He wanted to love God, wanted to *feel* loved by God. But he couldn't. He couldn't believe that God could love him, because he had done some serious stuff, and he just felt too guilty. He knew his sin was a problem that had to be taken care of.

Not long after, I met and became friends with a guy who had just become a pimp. He moved to Vegas, got into the nightclub and strip club scene, started meeting girls, realized there was money to be made, and became a pimp. His wife found out he was sleeping with the girls he was selling, and she walked out with their two kids. When we met, he was also crying. Just like the guy I had breakfast with, he thought he was too guilty to be forgiven.

I explained to each of them, "God loves you so much he wants to forgive your sin so he can have a relationship with you. He hates your sin so much he had to punish it. But he loves you so much he took the punishment himself."

I shared Bible verses, like Romans 4:25: "He [Jesus] was handed over to die because of our sins, and he was raised to life to make us right with God," and 1 John 1:9: "If we confess our sins to him, he is faithful and just to forgive us our sins and to cleanse us from all wickedness," and Ephesians 1:7: "He [God the Father] is so rich in kindness and grace that he purchased our freedom with the blood of his Son and forgave our sins."

I told them yes, you're guilty, and yes, you need help. But you have a friend who took care of your problem for you. Now you just need to call on him. God's offered to take away your guilt, but a gift isn't yours until you accept it. If you believe and say yes, you'll be forgiven and God's love will flood into your life and you will be free.

And the guy who had just been in prison . . . didn't. I don't know if he just couldn't believe it, or if he just refused to receive it, but he never said yes. We met repeatedly, he came to our church a few times, but he never said yes. And I think his life is the same today as it was back then.

The guy who had ruined his life and his family by becoming a pimp . . . did. He believed, and he said yes. We kept meeting, he came to our church regularly, and his life completely changed. He quit taking advantage of girls. He restored his marriage and became a great husband and dad. He's now changing the lives of other people. His life has become pretty amazing, pretty beautiful.

You

We've all sinned, and it leaves us feeling guilty and dirty. We want to be clean. I think we're all desperate for forgiveness.

Have *you* said yes? Have you accepted Jesus' death as the substitute for the punishment you deserve?

You may be nodding your head, but have you *truly* embraced God's forgiveness?

Do you sometimes wonder if God can really use you in any significant way, because of all the things you've done wrong?

When you sin, do you feel too guilty to pray, instead of feeling drawn to talk to God to express how grateful you are for his forgiveness?

Does trying to live for God feel like a heavy burden to you, instead of "easy and light"*?

When something goes wrong, do you suspect God might be paying you back for something you've done?

If so, you haven't fully embraced God's forgiveness. And you need to know that while God is perfect, he is *not* a perfectionist. He is perfect, but he is also perfectly compassionate. He loves you, and you have this promise: "If we confess our sins to him, he is

---

* See Matthew 11:30.

faithful and just to forgive us our sins and to cleanse us from all wickedness."*

And when you truly embrace that, you'll be transformed by it. Your life will become pretty amazing, pretty beautiful.

• • •

Now What?

➤ Read Romans 4:23–5:11.

➤ Get a piece of paper and write down all the things that you feel guilty about. Look over the list. Confess it all to God. Burn the paper. That guilt is gone.

➤ Now write a thank-you note to God for loving you and dying so you could be forgiven. Rejoice that you have been declared not guilty and made right with God.

---

* 1 John 1:9.

Day 4

HOPE TO CARRY ON

*I pray that God, the source of hope, will fill you completely with
joy and peace because you trust in him. Then you will overflow
with confident hope through the power of the Holy Spirit.*

ROMANS 15:13

THERE'S A MOVIE PORTRAYING THE LIFE OF CHRIST, simply called
the *JESUS* film. It's been translated into all kinds of languages,
and millions of copies have been distributed throughout the world.
Paul Eshleman, one of the people responsible for that, tells about
when the movie was shown at a refugee camp in Mozambique.
Most of the people watching had never heard about Jesus. As they
watched the film portraying his life, they fell in love with him.
Then came the part when Jesus was arrested, beaten, and led away
to be crucified. Everyone began to weep and wail, and many rushed
toward the screen. Their cries and the dust they stirred up made
it impossible to finish the film, so the projector was turned off.
And for more than thirty minutes, the townspeople were on their
knees weeping.

They had lost hope.

And our hearts need hope.

Paul Eshleman explains that eventually the *JESUS* film crew settled the people down and turned the movie back on so they could know the end of the story. Jesus' story does not end in death on a cross, but in resurrection and new life. Jesus conquers death and walks out of the grave on the third day. And not only does he experience new life, he offers it to anyone who says yes.

When the townspeople saw how the story ended, the crowd exploded. They began cheering, jumping up and down, dancing, and hugging each other.

Nearly everyone made the decision to accept Jesus into their lives as the one who could take away their sins through the sacrifice he made. The following Sunday, five hundred new believers showed up at the church service offered for them.

When, as a nonbeliever examining Christianity, I first encountered the story of the Resurrection, I realized it was the critical piece my brain needed. I wanted to know if I could trust the message of the Bible, and this was the key historical incident I could use to prove it true or false. I soon learned there was all kinds of evidence proving the Resurrection actually happened, and I surrendered my life to Jesus. As someone who required proof, I am thankful God made a verifiable historical incident like the Resurrection the crux of our faith.[*]

I later realized that the Resurrection was also the critical piece my heart needed. Our hearts need hope. We are desperate for it. People say hope is like oxygen for the soul. Many lose hope, and they're suffocating without it.

As we look at this world, we despair at the condition it's in. The crime, the hatred, the economy, the wars, the environment—all the problems.

And sometimes we look at our own lives, and we despair at the condition *we're* in. The times we've screwed up, the relationships

---

* See 1 Corinthians 15:12-19.

we've ruined, how little progress we seem to be making, the fact that someday we're going to die.

And then something bad happens, and that's when the despair really hits the fan. I think of when I got a phone call in the middle of the night from one of my best friends, Rich. His teenage daughter Megan had been in a car accident. She was dead. I raced over to the house and grieved with Rich and his wife, Karen.

About ten years later, I received another phone call. Rich had a brain tumor. The cancer was aggressive. He didn't have much time. Last year Rich died.

I think of Karen. How do you lose your daughter and your husband and not lose your mind? How do you carry on? Is there any way to hold on to hope? Without it, would she just suffocate?

In Brennan Manning's book *Ruthless Trust*, he tells the story of John Kavanaugh, a man who volunteered for three months with Mother Teresa's ministry to the dying in Calcutta, India. He wanted to know how he should spend the rest of his life and hoped Mother Teresa could give him the answer.

When he met her, she asked, "What can I do for you?" Kavanaugh requested prayer. Mother Teresa asked, "What do you want me to pray for?"

This was what he came for, the moment he had waited for. He answered, "Pray that I have clarity."

"No," she said, "I will not do that." He was confused and asked why. She replied, "Clarity is the last thing you are clinging to and must let go of."

This wasn't what Kavanaugh was hoping for. He countered that she always seemed to have the kind of clarity he was longing for. She laughed and said, "I have never had clarity; what I have always had is trust. So I will pray that you trust God."

The question we all need to wrestle with is this: Are we hoping for something or are we hoping in someone?

If we're hoping for something—the career we dream of, financial security, a perfect family—we're sure to be disappointed.

But if we're hoping in someone and that someone is Jesus, who loved us enough to go to the cross, and was strong enough to walk out of the grave, ultimately we'll never be disappointed.

Rich's daughter Megan died around midnight . . . on Easter Sunday. I was at his house till about four in the morning, then went home and rewrote my sermon to include Megan's death in it. A few hours later I was standing in front of a room full of people explaining that yes, Megan had died, and the sadness felt overwhelming. But I also explained that we do "not grieve like people who have no hope. For since we believe that Jesus died and was raised to life again, we also believe that when Jesus returns, God will bring back with him the believers who have died."*

Our hope, when we despair at the condition of the world or at the condition we're in, or even when tragedy strikes, is certain, because our hope isn't in something; it's in someone.

That doesn't mean we don't get confused. We often live without clarity. But the one thing we can have is trust. We can trust in God. And he can give us the hope our hearts hunger for, the hope we need to carry on.

•   •   •

Now What?

> Read 1 Peter 1:3-9.

> That passage tells us we can live with hope. We get so caught up in the things of this world and so depressed by our problems, but it's all temporary, and we have the

---

* 1 Thessalonians 4:13-14.

certainty of a better future in heaven. A pastor once tried
to help his kids learn this lesson by having them stamp
the word "temporary" on all of their belongings. You might
not want to literally stamp your stuff, but why not mentally
stamp "temporary" on all your belongings and on all your
problems today?

> Prayer can be used to repent. To repent means to change
your mind and your direction. Ask God to show you what
you've been putting your hope in. One way to detect it is
by filling in the blank: "I would be happy if _____."
What do you think you need? Whatever it is, pray and
repent. Ask God to help you change your mind and become
sure that the only thing you really need is him.

Day 5

SEEKING A STORY

The wisdom we speak of is the mystery of God—his plan that was previously hidden, even though he made it for our ultimate glory before the world began.

1 CORINTHIANS 2:7

"What's the meaning of life?"

"What's my purpose?"

"Isn't there more to life than this?"

Many people ask those questions. They ask those questions a lot. Maybe you've asked those questions.

Why?

I believe we're all seeking a story. Intrinsically we know that life makes sense only if it has a story line, and that our lives matter only if they're part of a bigger story.

Can you imagine watching a movie or reading a novel and realizing halfway in that it has no story line? There's no plot, no sequence to the random scenes, nothing significant is going to happen. You'd be annoyed that your time was wasted, and you'd want your money back.

Some of us feel that way about our lives.

Maybe this is why we love stories—in movies, in novels, in a great David-versus-Goliath sporting event. Why are we so drawn to a great story? I think it's because we sense that a great story is missing in our lives.

Your Story

It's not that you don't have a story. You do. It's inescapable. We all choose story lines for our lives.

Maybe you choose the story of individualism. With Frank Sinatra's "I Did It My Way" as your theme song, you've decided that no one will tell you what to do. You won't live for others or seek to meet their expectations. You're an individual.

Or maybe the story of consumerism is your pick. With "Whoever dies with the most toys wins" as your motto, you're sure that if you get enough, you'll be satisfied. What people seek to consume will vary, but the story line remains the same. It could be promotions, sexual conquests, bigger houses, nicer cars, more vacations, or a constant sense of fun and excitement. Whatever it is, you're trying to get as much as you can.

It's probably not as common as it used to be, but you might choose the story of nationalism. Your country's flag is your symbol, your nation gives you your identity, you listen to lots of news, and you live and die with the Olympic standings.

A surprising number of people will take on the victim's story. If that's your story line, nothing ever goes right for you. You've been taken advantage of and walked over. Every relationship you've had has fallen apart, and it's never been your fault.

Maybe you opt for the story of the American dream. You just want to be happily married, have a dog, and raise 2.5 kids who grow up to be successful. You don't ask for much—just to live in a nice home and go on nice vacations.

Perhaps you choose the story of religion. You want to be a nice person. You try hard to do good deeds and not to sin. You want to earn the approval of God. But earning God's approval is not the story God authored. In fact, that story line is kind of the opposite of what the Bible teaches Christianity is about.

Metanarrative

Here's the problem: all of those stories are too small. Way too small. Choose one of those story lines, and you find yourself asking, "Is this all there is?" and "Isn't there more to life than this?"

It's like putting together a puzzle. You dump out the contents of the box and have what seems to be a bunch of random pieces. Pick one up and it will seem haphazard, even meaningless. Then you look at the box. You see the big picture, and it enables you to see how all the individual pieces fit together and are part of the whole.

We need a picture on the box to make sense of our lives.

Philosophers call it a metanarrative. *Meta* meaning "beyond"; *narrative* meaning "story." The idea is that there are all kinds of stories weaving their way through history, and we each have our individual stories we add to the mix, but there has to be one big story that reaches beyond the individual stories and makes sense of them all. Without a metanarrative, history is unexplainable and our lives don't make sense. We need that central story.

So what is God's bigger story that we find ourselves in? We'll get into it in more depth in our next section, but here's a CliffsNotes version.

The story starts with God. God is love.* And God has always lived in a perfect love relationship with himself. That may sound odd, but the Bible teaches that God is three distinct persons—Father, Son, and Holy Spirit—who live in such a tight-knit community of love that they exist as one. One God who has always existed in a perfect humble community of affection and intimacy and mutual submission and serving.

---

* See 1 John 4:8.

Then God decided to create. He made a universe, including the earth and people to live on it.

He made you.

Why?

So he could share his love. So he could bring others into his perfect, humble community of affection and intimacy and mutual submission and serving.

But there was a problem. The people God created rejected his love, the love they were made for, and refused to live in the perfect, humble, intimate, mutually submissive, and serving way he wanted.

It turns out God is so loving that he didn't give up on people but continued to reach out in love to them and lead them toward his way of living.

But people are so rebellious that they continued to reject God's love and rebel against his way of living.

So . . . God came himself, in human form. Not to punish people, as they deserved, but to show and to teach what a life and a community of love could look like.

The people responded by . . . killing God.

But God is so powerful that death could not hold him down. After dying, he came back to life.

And he is so loving that he counted his death as the punishment people deserved for their rebellion against him, his love, and his way of living.

God is still reaching out to people. He's still making the offer that people can live in his love and learn how to live life his way and live in his kind of community.

When people accept that offer, they get to start experiencing that now, and after this life they will fully experience it when they join God in heaven.

People who accept the offer join God in his mission of inviting others to share in his love and in his way of doing life and community so that their stories can make sense too.

God is still creating. He promised he's making a place for us to live with him, in his love and his kind of community, as he originally intended.* One day he's going to come again, this time to bring us to that place. And there your story—all of it: the pain, the joy, the mystery—will make perfect sense.

• • •

Now What?

> Read Galatians 4:3-7.

> A new, and very significant, chapter of God's story started when Jesus came to our world to live among us. And he came so you could be adopted as his child! You were a part of God's plan from the beginning. How do you see your life fitting into God's story? What changes do you need to make so your life could better fit with God's story line?

> Try praying with your imagination today. Imagine the life you've led was made into a movie. What parts would you be embarrassed about? Would it be boring? Would you be the kind of person people would want to root for? Next, ask God to show you what your "movie" could be like if you let him become the writer and director of it. What changes might he make? Will you let him actually make those changes?

---

* See John 14:1-4.

WEEK TWO
Story

We love great stories in movies and in novels.

*Maybe part of what we need is to
find ourselves in a great story.*

*What is God's story? What is the overarching
story of the Bible? What does it have to do with
us? How do we fit into it? Could merging our
stories with God's story change our lives?*

Day 1

GOD

Everything comes from him and exists by his power and is
intended for his glory. All glory to him forever! Amen.

ROMANS 11:36

A FEW YEARS AGO I SAW A MOVIE where the main character says he feels like life is a movie, and he's the star of it.* Everyone else— his neighbors, coworkers, family members, the waitress at the restaurant—are just supporting actors making occasional cameo appearances in the movie about his life.

The idea would be kind of clever and funny if it didn't hit so close to home.

Do you feel like the star of your story? Does it seem like your family and friends have been included in it to support you? And the waitress and garbage man and grocery clerk exist to serve you?

We would never say it like that, but most people think that way. And can I suggest it's why most people go through life mostly sad?

There's a little problem with the way we tend to think.

It's all wrong.

Life is a story, but it's not about you.

God is the star of the story.

---

* Let's ignore the irony that this was said in a movie by the actor who was, indeed, the star of the movie.

Life: Starring God

It's all about God.

If you kind of think of yourself as the center of the universe, this idea will bother you, but it's all about God.

It's always been all about God. In fact, in the beginning, there was only God. Now don't picture God being lonely, because he wasn't. As I've mentioned, God has always existed in perfect community. He is three, yet one. The word *Trinity* is often used to describe this idea. God is three distinct beings who live in such tight-knit, loving, bonded community that they exist as only one being, one God. One God made up of three persons: God the Father, God the Son, and God the Holy Spirit.

God is the star. And somehow, despite being God, God is so humble that each member of the Trinity tries to make the others the stars. We see God the Father glorifying his Son Jesus.* We see Jesus glorifying his Father.** We see the Holy Spirit of God glorifying God the Son.*** God is so humble that each member of the Trinity tries to defer glory to the other members of the Trinity. But make no mistake, God is the star of the story.

And God decided to create. He created a universe, an earth. Why? "The heavens declare the glory of God; the skies proclaim the work of his hands."**** The creation glorifies the Creator. Nature points to God, because he is the star of the story.

God also decided to create people. Why? God says, "I have made them for my glory."***** In fact, we're commanded, "Whether you eat or drink, or whatever you do, do it all for the glory of God."****** And we're given this blessing: "May you always be filled with the fruit of your salvation—the righteous character produced in your life by

---

* See, for instance, John 8:54 and Matthew 3:16-17.
** See, for instance, John 12:28; John 14:13; John 17:1-4.
*** See, for instance, John 16:13-14.
**** Psalm 19:1, NIV.
***** Isaiah 43:7.
****** 1 Corinthians 10:31.

Jesus Christ—for this will bring much glory and praise to God."*
We exist to glorify God. We're to point our lives at him and honor
him as the star of the story.

Who Will Be the Star of Your Story?

So the question you and I have to answer, not just one initial time,
but a thousand times every day, is: Who will be the star of my story?
Will I live my life and make decisions to try to glorify myself, or
will I seek to bring glory to God in everything I do?

You may think living your life for God's pleasure instead of for
your desires might lead you to a smaller life, but exactly the opposite
will happen. Your life will be so much bigger and so much better.

In his book *Disciple: Getting Your Identity from Jesus*, Bill Clem
gives a great illustration of this:

Imagine two drama students, each with a dream of making it
big as an actress.

One day the first drama student comes up with a plan. She decides
to create her own play with a starring role for herself. Though she's
never written, she starts working on a script. Once it's completed,
realizing that she can't afford to pay other actors, she enlists two of
her friends to take the other roles. She doesn't have money to rent
a venue or create staging, so she talks her parents into allowing the
play to be performed in their garage.

The second drama student auditions for a small part in a big
Broadway play in New York. She gets the part. It's a minor role, but
she'll be working with some of the best actors, acting coaches, direc-
tors, and producers in the industry, and an outstanding playwright
wrote the script.

Which student do you think will have the more significant experience? My money is on the one in the Broadway play: she may have
a small role, but she is part of something much bigger than she could

---

* Philippians 1:11.

ever hope to create on her own. The girl in the garage, on the other hand, is trying to convince herself that she's constructed something worth being a part of. But, in reality, she has constricted herself to a very small story played out in a very small setting.

When you choose to live your own story, it's very small. Because you are the star of it, you may think it's a big deal, but it's really not.

But when you choose to find yourself in God's story and make him the star of it, you become a part of something huge. Your life will be, and it will feel, much bigger and more important, because you're no longer the most important person in the story.

Are You Sure God Is the Star?

Some people choose to construct and live out their own stories. Then at some point they invite God into their stories. They'll tell you, "I invited Jesus into my life." But honestly, the way they live their lives reveals that it's still their story.

God's not proposing that we invite him into our lives. He's asking us to *give* him our lives. We surrender our lives to God's will and to living for his glory. We say, "I want to be a part of God's story. And even if I just get a bit part, that's okay, because I'm still part of the BIG story. Because pleasing and bringing glory to God is the most significant thing I can experience, that's what I want to do with my life."

• • •

Now What?

> Read Colossians 3:1-17.

> How does this passage describe a life lived for God's glory? What do you think would need to change for your life to better point to and glorify God as the star of the story?

➤ Tell God that he is the star of your story. Admit to him your fears about that and the ways you feel inadequate to actually live that way. Ask him for help!

Day 2

GOD IS COMING FOR US

A child is born to us, a son is given to us. The government will
rest on his shoulders. And he will be called: Wonderful Counselor,
Mighty God, Everlasting Father, Prince of Peace.

ISAIAH 9:6

I'M GOING TO ADMIT SOMETHING. I don't want to, but I want to
have a transparent relationship with you. So here goes: growing up,
I watched *The Brady Bunch*. I watched a lot of *The Brady Bunch*.*

I loved the Brady family. I felt like Greg and Peter and Bobby
were my brothers. Marcia, Jan, and Cindy were my sisters. Tiger
was my dog, Alice my maid, and Sam my butcher.**

There was one episode when Greg got locked in Sam-the-
butcher's meat cooler. It looked like he was going to die. What
drama! What if Greg froze to death in Sam's meat cooler? Can
you imagine how the opening song would have gone after that
episode? "Here's the story . . . of a man named Brady. Who had
three sons, but one froze to death in Sam's meat cooler. Now only
three men, living with their grief, Greg's become a chunk of beef.

---

* Let him who hath not watched *The Brady Bunch* cast the first stone.
** It took years of therapy to fix this.

The Bradys' lunch. The Bradys' lunch. That's how Greg became the Bradys' lunch."

Greg was in serious trouble in that meat cooler. I watched, and I loved Greg, and I wanted so badly to enter my television, to go right into it and save him. But I felt so powerless.

Greg just stayed in his horrible situation and waited for someone to save him.

Heaven, We Have a Problem

There is a story. God is the star of the story.

God is also love.*

God is love and lives in a perfect community of intimacy and mutual submission and serving. So God decided to create people with whom he could share his love and community.

But there was a problem. The people God created rejected his love and refused to live his way and in his kind of community. It started in the beginning in the Garden of Eden, and it's continued throughout history with every person's decision to sin.**

Yet it turns out that God's love is so great, he doesn't give up on us.

That's one of the things we see in the Old Testament of the Bible.

In the Old Testament, God reveals the standard for being in relationship with him. He gives the law, including, most famously, the Ten Commandments, setting the standard he expects for our behavior. In a sense, what God is doing is asking us to live and treat each other the way God the Father, the Son, and the Holy Spirit have always lived and treated each other. It's the way God has

---

* Note that I didn't say God is lov*ing*. The Bible says that God is love (1 John 4:8). If it said God is loving, that would be a characteristic of God. Like you could say that I am loving because, well, most of the time I am. But it says that God *is* love. That means love is what he *is*. Like I am human. Being human defines me. I can't not be human. Love defines God. He can't not be loving.

** People toss the word *sin* around without knowing what it means. One of the words the Bible uses for *sin* was originally an archery term. It means "to miss the mark." A person aiming an arrow at a bull's-eye but missing would have "sinned." God has a bull's-eye for us, a way he created us and intended for us to live. Jesus says that way is to love God and love people. It's to live the way God has always lived—in perfect intimacy, mutual submission, and serving. When we choose not to live that way, it's sin.

always done life, and he's not going to lower his standards to be in relationship with us.

But there's a problem. God won't lower himself to our standards to be in relationship with us, but we're incapable of living up to his standards to be in relationship with him. We have to keep the law to be in relationship with God, but we can't keep the law. The apostle Paul writes, "No one can ever be made right with God by doing what the law commands. The law simply shows us how sinful we are."* So the law God gives in the Old Testament doesn't lead us into a relationship with God; it leads us to see how far we are from God and that we're incapable of living his way on our own. If we want God, it turns out we need help.

In the Old Testament, God also reveals the consequence for violating the standard, for our wrong behavior. The consequence is death. It's been that way from the beginning, when God told Adam and Eve that if they sinned, they were sure to die.**

We think of dying as losing life. You stop breathing and your brain stops functioning and you're lying on the ground lifeless. But death also carries the connotation of separation. When a person dies physically, that person's soul is separated from his or her body.

God created us to live in his love and in his community, and if we rebel against the way he wants us to do life, we die, in the sense that we're separated from experiencing his love and life in his community.

Think of it this way: imagine I allow someone to come live in my house with my family. I explain the rules of the house. In our family, we treat one another with kindness. We don't lie to one another. We each pitch in and each do some of the chores. But let's say this guest refuses to live by my rules. Day after day he brazenly disregards the way our family does life together. Wouldn't it be fair

---

* Romans 3:20.
** See Genesis 2:17.

for me to tell this person that he's lost the privilege of living with us? That his choices are forcing us to separate? Of course it would.

In the same way, God gives us life. The reason for our existence is to glorify him, to experience his love, and to enjoy his kind of life and community. If we refuse to live the way he asks, wouldn't it be fair for God to tell us that we've lost the privilege of living with him? That our choices lead to our being separated from him and his community of love?

We learn that the penalty for sin is death—not so much meaning a loss of life, but a separation.

This is why when Adam and Eve sinned, they didn't fall over lifeless. Instead, they had to leave the Garden where God was living in fellowship with them. They were walking, but they were dead. They were, for the first time, experiencing separation from God.

The consequence of sin is death, separation from God. There will come a time when we experience physical death—our souls will be separated from our bodies. And after that we will experience a third death—the eternal separation of our souls from God.

None of that is good.

We need help.

We need someone who can save us from ourselves, from our sin, and from the situation we put ourselves in.

The good news is that God sent Jesus to save us.

I watched that Brady Bunch episode and I couldn't stand the situation Greg had gotten himself in. He couldn't do anything to save himself, so all he could do was wait and hope.

I watched and wanted to enter my TV and save him, but I couldn't.

God saw that humans had gotten themselves in a horrible situation. They couldn't do anything to save themselves. In the Old Testament we see them just waiting and hoping.

God couldn't stand the situation we had gotten ourselves into. He loved us despite our sin. And what I was powerless to do, God was able to do. I couldn't enter Greg's world to save him, but God could enter ours. So Jesus came into our world. He came to save us.

•   •   •

Now What?

> Read Isaiah 53:1-12.

> This was written hundreds of years before the birth of Jesus, yet it is an amazing foretelling of Jesus' life and what he would come to do for us. What do you see in Isaiah 53 that makes you think of Jesus?

> Confess to God the ways in which you've made poor choices and not lived by his rules. Let him know that you recognize your need of his forgiveness.

Day 3

GOD HAS COME FOR US

Christ is the visible image of the invisible God. He existed before

anything was created and is supreme over all creation.

COLOSSIANS 1:15

WHEN MY KIDS WERE YOUNGER, they wanted a pet. We said no. They begged for a pet. We told them we love other people's pets.

Finally we caved, but not much. We bought each kid a goldfish. Our son, Dawson, who was five at the time, named his Darth Fishy. Our daughter, Marissa, who was about to turn three, named hers Mackenzie.

We got home, dropped the fish in their tanks, and put the tanks on the shelf. The kids looked at them, looked at us, looked at them, looked at us, and walked away to watch TV. So much for the excitement of having pets.

Later Marissa said, "A fish isn't a very good pet." I asked why, and she explained, "Because you can't really love it, and it doesn't really love you back."

"Well," I tried to encourage her, "you can sort of love it."

Around that time we started to notice Mackenzie's tank always had dirtier water than Darth Fishy's. We couldn't understand it, until I walked in one day and found Marissa . . . petting her fish. Wanting to show her fish love, turns out she was trying to pet it a few times a day.

Her fish didn't like it. In fact, her fish would panic and try to get away from the gigantic hand.

I wondered if maybe at night, after we all went to sleep, her fish would get out its diary and write, "It happened again today. It was a normal day, intermittent light, 72 degrees, pink gravel beneath me. I was trying to decide, should I swim towards the surface or bottom, swim right or left, when suddenly it appeared—the shadow. The shadow is always the first sign that it's coming. Then it arrived, five enormous protruding limbs and a meaty paw trying to crush me. But I will not be destroyed by it! I did everything I could to get away! It did trap me in a corner and touch me, but only for a second. Then from somewhere in the heavens, I heard a thundering noise."

And the thundering noise was, of course, Marissa yelling, "Daddy, I just petted my fish!"

Resistant to Love

Have you ever thought about what it's like to be God? The Bible tells us that God is love and created us in love and for love.

But very quickly there was a problem in God's creation: these humans were resistant to love, and they didn't do well at loving God back. It wasn't so much that they didn't want love, because they did. But much of the time they didn't recognize it; much of the time they tried to get away from it.

All through the Old Testament we see God trying to share his love with people, and consistently people running from God and rejecting his love. In the last book of the Old Testament God says, "I have always loved you," then, "But you retort, 'Really? How have you loved us?'"*

---

* God uses the prophet Malachi as the go-between for this conversation. We find this part of it in Malachi 1:2.

I can imagine God thinking, *How have I loved you? I've done everything for you! How else could I love you? What can I do to get you to accept my love?*

And it was almost as if God had an idea.*

God Came for Us

Watching my daughter try to love her fish, I felt so bad for her. She just wanted to show love, but no matter what she did, her fish would not accept it as love. She would try to pet the fish, and it would run away as if Freddy Krueger were after it. There was just no way for Marissa to connect with and communicate love to her fish.

But what if there were some way for Marissa to get in the tank? If she could somehow become a fish, she could show her fish love in a way it could understand. That might actually work.

God's idea was to get in the tank. To become like the ones he loved, so he could communicate his love.

This is described in the book of John, where Jesus is referred to as "the Word." The book of John begins by explaining that Jesus was with God and was God from the beginning: "In the beginning was the Word, and the Word was with God, and the Word was God. He was with God in the beginning. Through him all things were made; without him nothing was made that has been made. In him was life, and that life was the light of all mankind. The light shines in the darkness, and the darkness has not overcome it."**

And then God jumped into the tank. "The true light that gives light to everyone was coming into the world."*** Jesus left heaven to come to the world.

Another passage in the Bible describes it this way: "Though he was God, he did not think of equality with God as something to cling to. Instead, he gave up his divine privileges; he took the

---

* God actually had this idea all along. It didn't really just occur to him.
** John 1:1-5, NIV.
*** John 1:9, NIV.

humble position of a slave and was born as a human being. . . . He appeared in human form."*

God became one of us. So when we look at Jesus, we see God. Jesus is exactly God and exactly what God is like. The Bible says "Christ is the visible image of the invisible God"** and "the Son is the radiance of God's glory and the exact representation of his being."***

That is kind of ironic, because some people say, "Yeah, I've read the Bible, and I like Jesus, but I don't like the God of the Old Testament." But they're actually exactly the same.

So why does there seem to be such a difference?

Well, why was Marissa's fish scared of her? Why, when Marissa put her hand in to pet her fish, did her fish flee as if its life were in danger? Because Marissa was just too big, too different, too above her fish for her fish to understand her love.

If Marissa could have gone into her tank as a fish and snuggled a little, maybe her fish would have understood her love. Her love wouldn't be any different; it would just be on a level her fish could understand.

Why did God become one of us? "God so loved the world that he gave his one and only Son."**** Jesus came because of God's love and to express God's love.

Murder in the Fish Degree

Think about this: What if Marissa became a fish and got in the bowl, but her fish didn't snuggle up and love her back? What if her fish killed her?

That's exactly what happened to Jesus. He got into our skin, came to the world, and the people he came to love killed him.

* Philippians 2:6-7.
** Colossians 1:15.
*** Hebrews 1:3, NIV.
**** John 3:16, NIV.

But that was part of God's plan as well.

It was part of God's plan, because God created us in love and for love. We exist to be in relationship with God. But we've all walked away from that relationship, and God had to create a way to bring us back to him. Jesus said, "I am the way."* God had to create a bridge to span the gap between us. Jesus is that bridge. God had to do something about the sin that stains us and separates us from a perfectly pure God. The Bible says that Jesus became sin for us and did away with all of our sin on the cross. It was all part of God's plan, because God created us in love and for love. And Jesus' coming and dying was the only way we could be in relationship with him.

● ● ●

Now What?

> Read Philippians 2:6-11.

> This passage describes the descent Jesus made from heaven to earth to the cross. What do you find in these verses to be thankful for? What do you find in Jesus that you should emulate?

> Thank God for Jesus. Thank him that Jesus was humble enough to become a human and loved you enough to die for you.

---

* John 14:6.

Day 4

GOD WANTS TO LIVE INSIDE US

Because we are his children, God has sent the
Spirit of his Son into our hearts.

Galatians 4:6

When my wife and I started dating, I was in law school in Illinois, and she was in college in Buffalo, New York.* Yes, it was the dreaded long-distance relationship. This was a time before cell phones,** when you had to pay for calls by the minute. Our phone bills rivaled the gross national product of some small countries. We couldn't afford them, but we were in love, and mushy feelings were involved, and we had to talk.

Even better were the occasional visits. She would take the train*** to visit me, or I would drive to see her. We would be together for a few days, and all would seem right with the world. But then we would separate and there would be weeping and talk of "I can't live without you" and "How will I live until I see you again?" and "Oh no, someone is bringing a cat on the train."

---

* We chose our colleges by our desire to live in tropical locations.
** It was a time when AT&T ruled the earth and pterodactyls soared through the sky. (And yes, that is how you spell *pterodactyl*. I can't believe it myself. Had to check it several times to become convinced.)
*** It was a time when people took trains, and *ER* soared in the TV ratings. (And yes, that is how you spell *ER*.)

Eventually, after several years of tortured dating, we got married. Finally we moved to the same place and were able to always and fully be together.

Moving

God, who had always lived in a separate place and had made only cameo appearances in burning bushes and clouds of fire, came to earth in the person of Jesus. God was now hanging out with people. Jesus was called "Emmanuel"—which means "God with us" and was a perfect nickname because it was perfectly and wonderfully true.

Then Jesus was crucified. To all who watched, not only was God dead, but he was no longer with us. His presence was no longer on earth.

But the story took an exhilarating turn when Jesus walked out of the grave. God was back. He was with us again!

Then the story took what seemed to be a bleak turn. Jesus announced he was leaving. He was going back to heaven.

This seems like an odd choice. If I were Jesus and I had risen from the dead, I would go to as many places as possible. I would want everyone to see that I was alive. I'd make appearances on *TODAY* and *The Tonight Show*. I'd have T-shirts printed up with "Jesus World Tour" on the front and the dates and cities where I'd be appearing on the back. But that's not what Jesus did. He rose from the dead, stayed forty days, appeared to hundreds of people (but not everyone), trained his disciples for ministry, and left.

His followers must have been heartbroken. But before he died, Jesus had told them something that should have been very encouraging: "You grieve because of what I've told you. But in fact, it is best for you that I go away, because if I don't, the Advocate won't come. If I do go away, then I will send him to you."*

* John 16:6-7.

Remember, God is one God who exists in three distinct persons—God the Father, God the Son, and God the Holy Spirit. "The Advocate" is a nickname for the Holy Spirit.

The idea is that God being with people wasn't over when Jesus left. Emmanuel was not going to end. The story of God is a story of his increasing intimacy with people. When Jesus left, it wasn't God moving away. God actually moved closer, because he moved inside of us, through his Holy Spirit.

And, Jesus says, it is actually better to have the Holy Spirit with us than to have Jesus with us.

Better?

Why is having the Holy Spirit in us better than having Jesus here?

First, because when Jesus was here, he lived as a human, and that involved some limitations. For instance, as far as we know, Jesus was never in two places at the same time. So if Jesus had stayed around forever and done a continual world tour, maybe you would get to see him once a year when he stopped in your town. But the Holy Spirit is not limited in that way, so you can be in the presence of God all the time.*

And it's not only that you get more time in the presence of God but also that the presence of God gets in *you*. During Old Testament times, God seemed distant. With the arrival of Jesus, people could see and touch God. But when Jesus left, God came much closer and became far more intimate. The Bible teaches that when people choose to give their lives to God, God gives his Holy Spirit to them. The Holy Spirit moves into and takes up spiritual residence in believers. So not only do we get to be in the presence of God all the time, but we also get the presence of God in us.

Having the Holy Spirit is also better because through his presence in us we get access to God's power. Jesus told his followers,

---

* It's also cheaper, since you don't have to buy the Jesus World Tour shirt.

"You will receive power when the Holy Spirit comes upon you. And you will be my witnesses, telling people about me everywhere—in Jerusalem, throughout Judea, in Samaria, and to the ends of the earth."* It's like Jesus knew the mission was too big for his followers, so he provided the Holy Spirit so they'd engage in the mission with God's power. And the mission God has for us—sharing Jesus with the entire world—is so big that we need God's power in us through his Holy Spirit.

It's not just the mission God has for us that requires God's power; so does the life God has for us. God has called us to live holy lives, and to put it mildly, that's not something we're good at. We have this human nature that pulls us toward sin. That's why God put *his* nature inside us. The apostle Peter writes,

> By his divine power, God has given us everything we need for living a godly life. We have received all of this by coming to know him, the one who called us to himself by means of his marvelous glory and excellence. And because of his glory and excellence, he has given us great and precious promises. These are the promises that enable you to share his divine nature and escape the world's corruption caused by human desires.**

Do you really need the Holy Spirit? If you want to live a holy life, you do. It's only through sharing in God's divine nature that we can overcome our human nature.

Power?

God has given us his Holy Spirit so we can have his power to live holy lives and carry out our mission. Now it's up to us to plug in to that power.

There are a bunch of verses instructing us to "be filled with the

---

* Acts 1:8.
** 2 Peter 1:3-4.

Holy Spirit" and to "walk by the Spirit."* The idea seems to be that having the Holy Spirit inside you doesn't necessarily mean you're accessing God's power. You need to stay plugged in.

How? We'll talk about that in days to come, but for now, congratulations! Reading the Bible and praying are two key ways we plug in, and you're doing that right now. Look at you, being all awesome!

Keep moving in the right direction, and remember, you are not in a long-distance relationship with God. He is always with you and even inside you, if you've chosen to become part of his story.

•   •   •

Now What?

> Read Galatians 5:16-26.

> This passage makes it sound like we have a war going on inside us, two sides each pulling us in opposite directions. How have you experienced that? What are some of the things you could do to "live by" the Holy Spirit and let him guide you?

> Without the Holy Spirit living inside you, you wouldn't have the power to live the life God has for you and that you really want to live. Thank God for the Holy Spirit, and ask him to help you to be aware of and reliant on the Holy Spirit all the time.

---

* See Ephesians 5:18 and Galatians 5:16.

Day 5

GOD IS COMING BACK

Christ was offered once for all time as a sacrifice to take away the sins of many people. He will come again, not to deal with our sins, but to bring salvation to all who are eagerly waiting for him.

<small>HEBREWS 9:28</small>

HAVE YOU EVER WATCHED A MOVIE AND THOUGHT, *Is this ever going to end?* Maybe it was boring or too long or just bad, and you couldn't wait for the final scene and the credits to roll.

Do you ever feel that way about life? It can become a little boring at times as we yearn for something more. Sometimes it seems to be going on forever. And there's so much that's just bad. We look at all the problems in the world, and we suffer through our own problems, and we wonder, *Is this ever going to end? Could we get a final scene, maybe a climactic ending?*

Yes. Yes, we can. And . . . we will.

I'll Be Back

Arnold Schwarzenegger, as the Terminator, famously promised, "I'll be back."* It became the catchphrase of 1984. Everyone was

---

* Please read with your best thick Austrian accent.

saying it.* But almost two thousand years before Arnold and all my annoying friends uttered those infamous words, Jesus made that guarantee. He said, "The Son of Man** will come with his angels in the glory of his Father and will judge all people according to their deeds" (Matthew 16:27).

I've read that once when the famous preacher Billy Graham was on *The Tonight Show*, the host, Johnny Carson, said to him, "You know, Billy, I was just thinking: I bet if Jesus came back, we'd do him in again. Wouldn't we?"

Billy Graham is said to have replied, "Well, Jesus is coming back. But no, we won't do him in. Because this time he's coming in power and in glory."

Jesus will be back. You'll hear people trying to predict when it will happen. Don't listen to them. Jesus said, "No one knows the day or hour when these things will happen, not even the angels in heaven or the Son himself. Only the Father knows."*** If Jesus didn't know when God the Father would have him return, some guy preaching on public-access television probably doesn't either. In fact, I think our not knowing is part of God's plan. Jesus more or less said so: "You also must be ready all the time, for the Son of Man will come when least expected."****

48 Hours

Let me ask you this: What would you do if you knew you only had forty-eight more hours to live?

Did you think, *I'd watch a lot of TV*? Or, *I'd go right to the mall and do a lot of shopping*? Or, *I'd get to the office and make sure I get a lot of work done*? Or, *I'd probably spend most of my time on Facebook*? Or, *I think I'd play video games*?

---

* In 1984 the band Wham! was popular, women were wearing leg warmers, and everyone thought *Knight Rider* was the coolest. The year 1984 may not have been humanity's best year.

** Jesus often referred to himself as the Son of Man. It was an allusion to verses in the Old Testament, including Daniel 7:13-14, where the Son of Man is pictured as coming with the clouds of heaven to establish his rule over every nation.

*** Matthew 24:36.

**** Luke 12:40.

I doubt it.

The funny thing is that we have no idea how much time we have left—it may be only forty-eight hours—but those are the ways most of us will spend our time. We live like we have forever, but Jesus says we should "be ready all the time."

If we had only forty-eight hours, my guess is we'd make sure we're right with God and prepared for what comes after this life, and we'd try to help everyone we can to be right with God and prepared for what comes after this life.

I think keeping that as our daily focus is part of what it means to be ready all the time.

The Fool

One time Jesus told a story* about a man who is making lots of money and looking forward to a leisurely retirement. Then God speaks to him and says, "You fool! You will die this very night. Then who will get everything you worked for?" Jesus adds, "Yes, a person is a fool to store up earthly wealth but not have a rich relationship with God."

Admittedly, this story isn't a warning about Jesus returning. It's a story warning about death, but the point is the same.

Fool is, I think, the most negative word God calls anyone in the Bible. What made this man a fool? He was a fool because he lived for today and didn't have the end in mind. He cared only about this life and had no thought of eternity.

Knowing we are going to die and Jesus is going to return, that the end is coming, we'd be fools to live only for today.

Be Holy

I did a study of the passages about Jesus coming back, and I noticed a theme. Here are a few examples:

---

* See Luke 12:16-21.

May the God of peace make you holy in every way, and may your whole spirit and soul and body be kept blameless until our Lord Jesus Christ comes again.

1 THESSALONIANS 5:23

Obey this command without wavering. Then no one can find fault with you from now until our Lord Jesus Christ comes again.

1 TIMOTHY 6:14

The day of the Lord will come as unexpectedly as a thief. . . . What holy and godly lives you should live.

2 PETER 3:10-11

The theme? Be holy.

To be holy basically means to be set apart for a purpose. When you decide to make Jesus your Savior and Lord, you are choosing to be set apart by God for his purposes. So you live the rest of your life for God and in obedience to his commands.

There are so many reasons to be holy: God deserves it. God commands it. Jesus died for our sins, and we don't want to sin anymore. We now know better. There's a better life for us to live. God gave us the Holy Spirit so we can be holy. We represent God and want to set a good example.

And here we have another: Jesus will be back. The Bible says it this way in 1 John 2:28: "Dear children, remain in fellowship with Christ so that when he returns, you will be full of courage and not shrink back from him in shame."

God loves us so much, he invited us into his story. And as the story comes to its climax when Jesus returns, we don't want to be embarrassed by the part we played in it. We want to feel confidence, not shame.

The End

God is the star of the story.

It's his story, but he loves us and invites us into it.

Sometimes when we're living in it, it can feel long, and we just want it to end.

It's going to.

Jesus is coming back.

•　　•　　•

Now What?

> Read 1 Thessalonians 4:15–5:4.

> If you knew Jesus was returning in forty-eight hours, what would you be sure to do before he came? Whatever that is, it must be important, so why don't you actually do it?

> Ask God to help you to live with the end in mind, to live in such a way that you wouldn't be embarrassed if he returned and found you in the middle of whatever it was that you were doing.

WEEK THREE
New

We are all about new things. We'd love to
get a new car, a new house, new clothes.
We get excited for a new movie or new book.

We work hard at making our bodies feel new—or at
least not quite so old. We work out; we go on diets; we
change the color of our hair, the shape of our chins . . .

Perhaps we just want to be new. Could
that actually be possible with God?

Day 1

A NEW YOU

Anyone who belongs to Christ has become a new person.

The old life is gone; a new life has begun!

2 CORINTHIANS 5:17

IN 2014, AMERICANS SPENT MORE THAN $12 BILLION on over 10 million cosmetic surgery procedures. Every year more people are having "work done." In fact, check this out: in 2014, buttock augmentations were up 86 percent over 2013. I didn't even know I could get my buttocks augmented! I've been accepting my buttocks as is for so long, I kind of feel like a fool.

And it's not just our bodies. In 2012, Americans spent about $284 billion renovating their homes.

Americans also bought 16.5 million new cars in 2014. If you just can't buy a new car, you can buy a spray bottle of "New Car Scent" fragrance. Personally, I don't think anyone is going to be fooled when you pull up in your 1977 Malibu Classic with duct tape covering one quarter panel and your 8-track tape player cranking Lynyrd Skynyrd. Your friend is like, "Bob, this car . . . smells so . . . new. Is it new? Did you just buy this?"

I don't think the reason for cosmetic surgery is that we don't like our bodies; it's that we don't like ourselves. People believe building a new house will satisfy them, but the reality is that only building a new life will give them what they're truly looking for. A new car might look better than your old one, but only a new life can get you where you want to go.

The reality is I need a new me. And you need a new you.

Remember the glut of "makeover" TV shows? We still have quite a few today, but for a while it seemed like they were on every channel. One of those shows was *Extreme Makeover.* Here's what they promised: "a real-life fairy tale in which their wishes come true, not just by changing their looks, but their lives and destinies." They got one thing right: that is what we need! We need to change our lives and our destinies, but we can't do that through plastic surgery, remodeling our homes, improving our wardrobes, or pimping our rides, no matter what our culture tells us.

God's Image

What's the reason for this longing we have?

I think it's because we were made in God's image. We were designed to live our lives reflecting who he is. That's why we get so frustrated by our bad choices and bad habits, the things that drag us down, make us mistreat people, and stress us out. We know we were intended for better, but somehow we've messed things up. And something inside us screams, "I want to be made new!"

And the good news is that *we can be.* Here's the promise we have from God: "Anyone who belongs to Christ has become a new person. The old life is gone; a new life has begun!"*

If a person makes the decision to belong to Jesus, that person is made new. The old is gone; the new has come.

That should fill you with hope. You can be made new! You can be transformed! You're not stuck! You can change! You don't have to live forever the way you are now!

---

* 2 Corinthians 5:17.

God wants to make you new. He wants you to be like him.

The good news of the Bible is that God loves you not as you should be, but just the way you are. The *great* news is that God loves you too much to leave you as you are, because there's something so much better for you. He wants to help you be who you should be, the new you you've longed to be.

Jesus lived a perfect life—a life of joy and happiness, a life beyond fear and worry, a life of love and compassion, a life without sin and selfishness. He was pure, peaceful, and purpose driven. He had an unmatched intimacy with God. While God isn't asking you to stop being you, he does want you to be a new you, a new you that is just like Jesus. The Bible says that as we live out our new identity, we'll see character traits like "love, joy, peace, patience, kindness, goodness, faithfulness, gentleness, and self-control"* growing in our lives.

A Confused Butterfly

Maybe you've become a Christian, but you don't seem to be becoming more like Jesus. The new you seems a lot like the old you. What's up with that?

I think the problem for some of us is that we don't understand the promise God has made us. Since we don't understand that we have a new identity, we're still living out our old one.

Imagine a caterpillar. This caterpillar is crawling around in the dirt. Why? Because that's what caterpillars do. But then this caterpillar goes through an incredible transformation in which it becomes something brand new: a butterfly. It's a new creation. The old life is gone. The new life has begun. Now that it's a butterfly, it can take flight and soar through the air. But I want you to imagine this butterfly . . . crawling around in the dirt. What kind of butterfly would crawl around in the dirt? Well, I guess only one who

---

* Galatians 5:22-23.

didn't realize it was a butterfly. A butterfly who thought it was still a caterpillar would continue to crawl in the dirt.

And I wonder if the reason you aren't living up to God's promise of you being a new person in Christ is because you don't understand your new identity. You're a new person, but you still think you're the old person. So you still find yourself crawling in the dirt, when you are capable of taking flight.

Understand this: if you've become a Christian, even if you are still struggling with your old ways, your old habits, your old sins, that is *not* the real you anymore.

The apostle Paul struggled with living the same old way even after he became a brand-new person. He writes about it in Romans 7. And what he concludes is interesting and important. He writes, "Now if I do what I do not want to do, it is no longer I who do it, but it is sin living in me that does it."*

Did you notice the distinction Paul makes? He's saying, "I know I'm struggling. I know that this sin is in me. But it is not me. I am a new person. I may struggle with things from my past, but I am not my past."

And you are not your past. You are not your sin. Sin is no longer the truest thing about you.

You are a new person.

God has made you a brand-new you.

•　　•　　•

Now What?

> Read 2 Corinthians 3:18.

> As a Christ follower, you have a new identity. Your new identity is Jesus' identity, and it should be becoming a

---

* Romans 7:20, NIV.

reality in your life "more and more." What could help you to remember and stay focused on your identity so you can live it out?

> We often get stuck thinking of ourselves the way we've always thought of ourselves. Ask God to show you the old identity you maybe haven't let go of yet and to help you believe you really are new in Christ.

Day 2

A NEW HEART

Rid yourselves of all the offenses you have committed,

and get a new heart and a new spirit.

EZEKIEL 18:31, NIV

I REMEMBER THE FIRST TIME I EVER STOLE ANYTHING. I was thirteen years old. There was a cassette tape I wanted at a record store. I decided to steal it. As soon as I made that decision, my heart started racing, my palms became sweaty, and my head started pounding. I became a nervous, guilty wreck. But I went for it. I looked around, grabbed the cassette tape, and put it in my pocket. And at that exact moment the theme song from *Miami Vice* (which was a popular show at the time) started playing on the store's sound system. I freaked out. I expected Crockett and Tubbs to come running in to bust me. But they didn't. I casually walked out of the store, and I got away with it. I still was flustered, and I felt pretty guilty, but I got away with it.

Not too much later, I tried to steal something again, and it wasn't that scary. Afterward I felt only a twinge of guilt.

Soon I was stealing things every time I went to the mall without even giving it a second thought. Guilt? Not a bit.

Hard Hearts

The Bible says that we have a heart problem. We have heart disease, and it's terminal. The Bible refers to it as a hardness of heart.* A hard heart is a heart that's cold, unresponsive, independent, and rebellious toward God.

How do we contract this disease? Little by little.

It starts when we learn, at an early age, to say no to God. It doesn't have to be an aggressive, outright no. Just ignoring God functions effectively as a no. Each time we say no, our hearts become less tender; it's like a steel layer of resistance slowly encases our hearts. Little by little we're less sensitive to God's voice, it's easier to say no, and we feel less guilt over our sin. Soon, sins we never could have imagined committing can become second nature, and God is no longer on our radar.

Transplant

Hardness of heart is life's most fatal disease, but fortunately, God has a cure. Turns out our hearts are so diseased that heart treatments are not enough to solve our problem. What we desperately need is a heart *transplant*. "Rid yourselves of all the offenses you have committed, and get a new heart and a new spirit."**

We need new hearts, and that's what God offers us. He promises, "I will sprinkle clean water on you, and you will be clean. Your filth will be washed away, and you will no longer worship idols. And I will give you a new heart, and I will put a new spirit in you. I will take out your stony, stubborn heart and give you a tender, responsive heart. And I will put my Spirit in you so that you will follow my decrees and be careful to obey my regulations."*** A new heart that's soft, loving, and responsive to God replaces the old, hard heart. God wants to make you a new you, and he starts by giving you a new heart.

That may sound like it's straight out of a fairy tale, but it's true.

---

* See, for instance, Ephesians 4:18, Mark 8:17, and Jeremiah 17:9.
** Ezekiel 18:31, NIV.
*** Ezekiel 36:25-27.

God really changes people, and the transformation begins with their hearts. You see it in people in the Bible, like Paul, who went from an angry Christian-killer to a loving Christian. He was a new person with a new heart. You see it in people like me. I'm not perfect, but I am a *completely* different person from the one I was the day before I put my faith in Jesus. Ask anyone who knew me!

Guard

There's a guy I go to lunch with once in a while who is so wise that I want to write down just about everything he says. He'll be talking, and I'll be thinking, *Wow, I really want to write that down. It is so wise. I want to remember it. But I think it would be weird to take notes while we're eating lunch. I'd probably look silly. But it's so good! But I don't want him to feel uncomfortable. Shoot! I've missed what he's been saying because I've been thinking about taking notes. Wait, do I have lettuce in my teeth?**

Can you imagine getting advice from not just a wise person, but from perhaps the wisest person who ever lived? And what if, in the midst of giving you advice, he suddenly said, "Above all else . . ." What? The wisest person ever is giving you his wisest advice? It's definitely time to take notes!

The king of wisdom, Solomon, wrote the majority of the book of Proverbs in the Bible. It's a book of wisdom. In this book there is one line where he says, "above all else." I'm going to show it to you. You might want to take notes. "Guard your heart above all else, for it determines the course of your life."**

So let's say you've made the decision to put your faith in Jesus and to get a heart transplant from God. That's great. But you're not done being concerned about your heart yet. You can stop worrying about your heart when you get to heaven. For now, you need to guard your new heart.

The problem in your past is that your heart became increasingly

---

* Have I mentioned I'm a little ADD?
** Proverbs 4:23.

hard every time you said no to God. Then you received a new heart, but your new heart will also become increasingly hard every time you say no to God.

There's a book in the New Testament called Hebrews that is almost entirely devoted to warning believers about the dangers of letting their new hearts grow cold and hard toward God again.

One time the church I was leading was going through a challenging time. We needed new staff but couldn't find the right people, our offerings were down, and we faced all kinds of other issues. I found myself stressed out and worrying constantly. One night it culminated in losing a lot of sleep.

The next morning I got up and did my daily Bible study. My reading was in Hebrews 3, which warns about having "a sinful, unbelieving heart that turns away from the living God."* And it was like I heard God asking me, "Vince, have I always been faithful? Can you believe in me, in who I am, not just in what you see me doing?" And I said, "Yes, God, I can." And he was like, "All right then—let's do this."

It's so easy to get into a tailspin of unbelief.

I need to guard my heart.

You need to guard your heart.

You can trust God. You can believe in him, in who he is, even when you can't see what he's doing.

And when he asks you to do something, always say yes.

•   •   •

Now What?

> Read Hebrews 3:7-15.

> The way our hearts grow hard is by ignoring or saying no to God when he speaks to us. What is something God has told

---

* Hebrews 3:12, NIV.

you to do (either in black and white in the Bible or with a personal whisper) that you have ignored or refused? Now that you realize that your "no" is not isolated but contributes to the condition of your heart, why don't you say yes right now? What will that yes look like for you?

> The Bible says we lack wisdom because we don't ask God for it.* Ask God to give you wisdom, specifically to make the kind of choices that will allow you to guard your heart.

* See James 1:5.

Day 3

A NEW MIND

Don't copy the behavior and customs of this world, but let God transform you into a new person by changing the way you think. Then you will learn to know God's will for you, which is good and pleasing and perfect.

ROMANS 12:2

IMAGINE FOR A MINUTE that you're sitting in the driver's seat of your car at the closest airport. You've been there before. You start driving home. As you make your way, without being aware of it, you will make dozens—maybe hundreds—of mental assumptions. You turn the key because you assume that will start the car. You step on the gas pedal because you know that makes you go forward. When you want to stop, you push the brake. As you drive down the road, you don't even look at the speed limit signs because you know the limit is thirty-five in the neighborhood and fifty-five on the highway. You know what exit to take without having to think about it; you know where to turn without really having to make the decision. You could almost do it all with your eyes closed.

But what if all kinds of things had been changed without your knowing? You step on the gas pedal, and your car slams to a stop. You hit the brake, and your car lurches forward. Turn your wheel right, and your car goes left. You get pulled over and say, "Officer, what's the problem?" He explains that you were going thirty miles over the speed limit. You say, "But it's thirty-five!" He says, "No, it's five." You get on the highway, but it doesn't take you where you think it will. You're driving down a road, and when the traffic light turns green, everyone comes to a stop. You try to go home, but the road you live on doesn't seem to exist.

That scenario sounds strange, but it's closer to reality than you'd ever imagine.

Your Mental Map

In your head you have a kind of map, a mental framework; some would call it a worldview. It's the way you think about things, what you believe, the assumptions you have about this world, and the values you hold.

How did you get it? Well, more or less the same way you developed the "map" that allows you to drive home from the airport without thinking. Some of that came by training and some by experience, and it's all become deeply ingrained in your mind.

Similarly, you've been trained to think and to have certain assumptions, values, and beliefs by your parents, your education, and the media. And you also have experiences that have led to your current worldview.

But there's a problem. A lot of what you believe is wrong. Things you assume to be true are actually lies.

Why? Because we live in the kingdom of Satan, and he is a liar. The Bible tells us that the devil is very real and has a real influence on our world. He's called the ruler of the "kingdom of the air" and "of this dark world."* And Satan lies. Jesus says, "He has always hated the truth, because there is no truth in him. When he lies, it is consistent with his character; for he is a liar and the father of lies."**

---

* See Ephesians 2:2 and 6:12, NIV.
** John 8:44.

It sounds weird, almost sounds like *The Matrix* movie, where people were living in a systematic deception but didn't know it. And that's not far from the truth. There are things we think are true, but aren't. And things we think are false, are true.

A Renewed Mind

This is why as God makes you a new you, he wants to give you a new mind. We read that God wants to "transform you into a new person by changing the way you think"* and that God wants to "renew your thoughts and attitudes."**

Why is this so important? Because your thoughts and values and assumptions are the very fabric of who you are. They make up the mental map you're living by every day. We need to start living by the truth. When we do, Jesus says, the truth will set us free.*** We need a renewed mind with new thoughts.

If the mental "map" you have in your head that allows you to drive from the airport to your house were suddenly changed—if the gas pedal braked and the brake pedal gave your car gas, the streets were all changed, etc.—it would be awkward, and you would have to hesitate instead of assuming. You'd repeatedly pause and ask, *Wait, do I have this right? I could get myself in trouble with a wrong move.* You also would buy and study a map that reflects the new reality you're living in.

In the same way, when you realize you're living in a world built on lies but God has real truth available for you, it's going to be awkward for a while. And if you're wise, you'll hesitate instead of assuming, and you'll start studying a map that reflects the new reality you're living in. God's given us this map in the Bible. So you'll pause and ask, *Wait, do I have this right?*

Like, *I think that I'm the center of my universe, and the goal of life is*

---

* Romans 12:2.
** Ephesians 4:23.
*** John 8:32.

to be happy. But is that right? So you'd study your new map, and you'd ask for direction, and you'd realize, *No, that's wrong. The truth is that God is the center of my universe, and the goal of life is to make him happy.*

Or, *I think I need to get promoted and make lots of money to be someone special. My parents taught me that, and I've always believed it. But is it true?* And you'd learn, *No, that's wrong! I'm special because God made me and loves me. I need to get my self-esteem from him and rest in his love.*

Or, *I believe that truth is relative. There's no such thing as absolute truth. What's right for you is right for you, but it might not be right for me. We each have to figure out what's true for us. But, hold on, is that right?* And you'd figure out, *That's not true! I've been working under a false assumption. If there's a universal God, then whatever he says is universally true. An absolute God can make absolute truth—truth that is true for everyone, everywhere, at all times.*

Or, *I feel like I can have sex before I get married. It's my body. We're two consenting adults. It's not hurting anyone.* But you now discover, *I've been wrong! My body belongs to God. God decides what I can do with it. And he says sex is just for marriage.*

Our minds need to be renewed. We need to develop a new map, a biblical framework, a godly worldview so that we see things the way God does and so that we align our thinking with truth. And when we do that, the place it will take us to is freedom.

• • •

Now What?

> Read Ephesians 4:17-32.

> What does this passage show about how critically important a person's way of thinking is? Where might your thinking need to be renewed?

➤ Changing your thinking can take time and be challenging. Ask God for help. Ask him to reveal lies you believe and to lead you to know and embrace the truth that will set you free.

Day 4

NEW EARS

Jesus replied, "I have already told you, and you don't believe me.
The proof is the work I do in my Father's name. But you don't
believe me because you are not my sheep. My sheep listen to my
voice; I know them, and they follow me.

JOHN 10:25-27

As you may remember, when my wife, Jennifer, and I first started dating, we lived in different states. Living at a distance, we didn't communicate at all. Sure, we could have talked on the phone or written letters, but we decided not to. Instead we basically ignored each other. And our relationship grew and grew. It seemed like every day we fell deeper in love, and our commitment to each other became stronger.

Did you read that last paragraph twice? It doesn't make any sense, does it? It doesn't make sense because it's not true. Of course we talked. And if we hadn't, our relationship certainly would not have grown. If we never communicated, our love wouldn't have increased; it would have become stagnant, at best.

Maybe you want to love God more and feel more loved by him, but you're rarely communicating with him. And if so, of course the relationship is not growing.

Or maybe you pray, you do talk to God, but it's a one-way conversation. Can you imagine if during our long-distance dating, I wrote letter after letter to Jennifer, but she never responded? If I never heard from her, I'd start to wonder, and I'd get discouraged. Some of us are talking to God but never listening. It could be that the idea of God talking to you sounds odd. But when you become a new you, you get new ears that are designed to hear God. You just need to believe, be still, and be aware.

Believe

Maybe you're of the belief that God *used* to talk to people but doesn't do that anymore. That's just something that happened back in Bible times. *Sure, God spoke to Abraham and Moses; that's the Bible. That kind of thing doesn't happen anymore, and especially not to someone like me.*

But that's not true. God is the God who speaks. Not just back then, but today. In fact, if God can't speak, he's not much of a god at all. That's the idea we get in the Bible: that any god who can't speak is no god worth speaking of. "What good is an idol carved by man, or a cast image that deceives you? How foolish to trust in your own creation—a god that can't even talk!"*

God can speak, and the Bible tells us we should expect to hear from him. But if we're going to, we need to believe that he is able to and wants to speak to us. If we don't believe, we won't have ears to hear.

Be Still

God may occasionally get our attention in an unmistakable way that just cannot be ignored. But far more often, God's voice is not so obvious.

There's a story in the Bible where God set up a meeting with

---

* Habakkuk 2:18. See also Psalm 115:4-5.

a guy named Elijah. Elijah showed up at the mountain where they were supposed to meet and was waiting for God to arrive, when suddenly a hurricane-like wind whipped through. Elijah thought God was in the wind. But the wind died down, and God was not in the wind. Then out of nowhere, an earthquake shook the entire mountain. Elijah thought, *Here's God. He's come in an earthquake!* But God was not in the earthquake. Soon an inferno exploded, and fire raged through the area. Elijah thought, *God is arriving in a ball of fire.* But the fire subsided, and God was not in the fire. Then a gentle voice whispered, "Elijah." And that gentle voice asked Elijah a question and went on to gently confront him about a problem that was so serious it had led Elijah to consider suicide.

God came in a gentle whisper. And when Elijah went down off the mountain and people asked him, "What was it like to meet God?" I think he probably replied, in a kind of stunned way, "He whispered my name. I could barely hear him. I had to be still just to hear it. He whispered my name."

God says, "Be still, and know that I am God."* I've heard stillness described as silence on the outside and surrender on the inside. We need to get silent so we can hear God's whisper, and we need to surrender our wills to his leadership so we're willing to do whatever he tells us. What might that look like for you? How could you create some regular time to get away from all the distractions? If you, in that silence, invited God to speak to you, how do you think he'd respond to that?

Be Aware

We need to believe that God can and wants to talk to us. We need to be still, creating regular times when we listen for God's voice. And

---

* Psalm 46:10.

we also need to be aware, because God may choose to speak to us when it's not on our schedule.

New moms develop supersonic hearing with their babies. They have this incredible awareness and will hear any noise their babies make, even if the moms are sleeping, or vacuuming, or sleep-vacuuming.*

If we want to hear from God, we need to be aware, all the time. We need to have ears to hear and be sensitive to anything he might be saying to us.

That's difficult. I find I can be pretty receptive to God when I'm at church or during the time I've set aside to spend with him in the morning. But the rest of the time, I've got my agenda, and it's easy to miss out on what God wants for me. And if I miss out on that, I'm missing out on a big part of what makes being a Christian a supernatural, dynamic, exciting adventure.

I miss out on the precious moments God has for me. Like when I'm playing with one of my children, loving them, and out of nowhere sense God saying, "This is the way I feel about you." Or when I'm talking to a friend who's sharing some struggles and God prompts me, "This would be a great time to invite them to church." Or when I'm worrying about a relationship in my life or my finances, and suddenly I feel God's presence with me, and it's like he's saying, "You can trust me; I'll take care of you."

When that kind of thing happens, it's amazing. And I think I've missed out on many of those amazing moments because I had my agenda and I didn't have ears to hear God. That's not the way it's supposed to be.

God wants to talk to you. And he wants to lead and guide and encourage and counsel you in a relationship that becomes a divine romance, and into a life that becomes a great adventure.

That's what we all want.

---

* It's sleepwalking, but for type-A personalities who can effectively multitask.

• • •

Now What?

> Read Psalm 25:1-6.

> Try a prayer practice called "Hands Down, Hands Up."
Sit with your hands palms down and mentally "put down"
everything that is weighing on you at this moment. Lay your
burdens and distractions down. Breathe them out, picturing
them leaving you as you turn them over to God. Then
turn your palms up, and breathe in. Take in God's love for
you. Listen for his whisper. Take a few minutes to do this,
perhaps alternating between having your palms up and your
palms down.

> Spend your prayer time being still, becoming aware of
God's presence, and doing the "Hands Down, Hands Up"
prayer practice.

Day 5

A NEW SPINE

Be strong and courageous! Do not be afraid and do not panic

before them. For the LORD your God will personally go ahead

of you. He will neither fail you nor abandon you.

DEUTERONOMY 31:6

DID YOU SEE THE MOVIE *We Bought a Zoo*? It's the story of a recently widowed dad and his two kids. The father, whose career has been as an adventure writer, buys a zoo*—a dilapidated, dysfunctional, little zoo. He gets his family and the zoo staff together and announces, "I would like to declare us all modern-day adventurers." Later, a while into this adventure, the daughter asks him, "How come you don't tell stories anymore?" Dad says, "Because we're living the story."

I think that's what we want. We want to be swept up in an epic story that provides an adventure.

I think that's part of what God wants for us as well. Throughout the Bible we see him calling people into his story. I wonder if God wants to get us all together and announce, "I would like to declare us all modern-day adventurers."

---

* The title of the movie might have given that away—not really a spoiler there.

Sounds good, but there's a problem.

The problem is fear.

I Can't Do That

Question: Where in the Bible do we see a person responding to God's call to a task with a smile and saying, "No problem. That sounds easy"?

Answer: nowhere.

God calls Noah, telling him, "It's not raining, there's no threat of rain, but I want you to build an ark. And I'm going to make you responsible for restarting the whole human race."

God calls Abraham, saying, "I want you to leave everything and go to a place. I'm not going to tell you where the place is, or what the place is, until you get there. Just go. And as a ninety-nine-year-old man, you're going to have your first child and start a family."

God calls Moses and says, "You've established a nice little life for yourself as a shepherd. But I want you to go back to Egypt, where you're wanted for murder, and I want you to demand that the king release all the Israelite slaves."

God calls Joshua, telling him, "I want you to lead this ragtag group of Israelites to conquer the city of Jericho."

God calls David to face a giant; he calls Esther to confront a king; he calls the disciples of Jesus to bring the message of God to the entire world.

God *never* calls people to play it safe. He calls them to play it dangerous. He always calls people to something bigger and beyond themselves, something they could never do on their own.

This is why I have to laugh when I hear people say, "Christianity is a crutch for weak people." Um, no. The problem is that true Christianity is too intimidating for most people. To be a Christian often requires us to go against the grain of popular culture. It may demand that we take a stand against fierce opposition. It asks that we give generously and live on less than we make. It tells us to defend the weak. It requires us to find ways to share with people a message that they may not want to hear. And God may ask us to do something specific that causes our hearts to grow faint. I've known people who felt led by God to quit high-paying jobs, to move to other countries, or to become voluntarily homeless so they could minister to the poor.

God never calls people to play it safe. He calls them to play it dangerous. The question is: Will you have the courage?

Twenty Seconds of Insane Courage

In *We Bought a Zoo*, the dad has a motto he lives by: "You only have to be courageous for twenty seconds." When the moment requires him to step up and say yes, or to step up and do the right thing, he steels himself to be courageous for just twenty seconds. It's how he met his wife. He was walking down the street, saw an attractive woman eating at a restaurant by herself, and thought, *I'd love to meet her, but I couldn't just have a conversation with a beautiful stranger. I'm not that kind of guy.* Then he thought, *Well, I can be that guy for twenty seconds.* So he went up and talked to her. He later realizes that all the good things that have happened to him are because he got his nerve up for twenty seconds. Now he's trying to teach it to his son. He tells the boy, "Sometimes all you need is twenty seconds of insane courage. Just, literally, twenty seconds of just embarrassing bravery. And I promise you, something great will come of it."

That's what *we* need. The nice thing is that we don't have to muster up courage from our own resources. When God makes us new, he gives us a new spine.

Want to hear something cool? The Hebrew word *ruach*, which is normally translated "spirit" in the Bible, also means "courage." So when God gives us his Spirit, he's not only giving us his power, he's also giving us his courage.* And "what is the point of having God's power if you lack the courage to actually use it?"**

We need to be always asking, "God, what do you want me to do today?" "God, what do you want me to do in this moment?" And often, the things God wants us to do are rather ordinary, uneventful things; things that require just a quiet faithfulness and don't force us outside our comfort zones. But there *will* be moments when you cannot play it safe, and you'll need to muster up twenty seconds of insane courage to say yes to whatever it is God is calling you to do.

So let me ask: What is God calling you to do?

Maybe God is calling you to serve in a new way, to find a way of volunteering according to the unique way he's wired you, so you can make a bigger impact with your life for him.

Or perhaps God is calling you to a new career path. You've known for quite a while that you're in the wrong job, but fear has held you back from making the necessary change.

Or God could be calling you to generosity. You hold on with iron fists to your money, and God's telling you to loosen your grip and to give generously back to him.

Or it could be that you have a secret sin. It's a sin that you've been hiding for a long time, and part of its power over you is that you're the only one who knows about it. And maybe you need to ask God to help you muster up twenty seconds of insane courage to confess that sin to a trusted friend and ask for help.

Or it could be someone *else's* sin. It might be that you need to have a conversation with a friend whom you've been avoiding because of fear.

Or perhaps the conversation you need to have is with your spouse, because maybe things haven't been the way they should be in your marriage, for a long time. The two of you haven't talked

---

* I learned this in Erwin McManus's book *Uprising*.
** Ibid.

about it; you're just kind of drifting, and not in the right direction. And you need to have the courage to bring it out in the open and get help so you start moving in the right direction.

Or could it be that you need to give your life to God? You've never said yes to making Jesus your Savior and Lord, and you're afraid, but you need to.

Starting right now, I would like to declare you a modern-day adventurer who can take on whatever God is calling you to do. God's *Ruach* can give you a boldness to go beyond yourself. Because you can't play it safe and please God.

• • •

Now What?

➤ Read Joshua 1:6-9.

➤ Joshua is being asked to lead God's people into the Promised Land. How many times does God have to tell Joshua to be strong and courageous or not to be afraid? What do you feel like God is asking *you* to do? Why might it be easy for you to be afraid? Get quiet and listen for God's voice. Is he telling you to be strong and courageous?

➤ Prayer isn't only us talking to God; it's a conversation, and God wants to speak to us as well. Ask God to speak to you today, showing you what he wants you to do and giving you the courage to do it.

WEEK FOUR
Abide

A lot of people think God wants us to be religious. He doesn't. What he wants is a relationship with us. His offer is to be with us, even in us, and his invitation is that we get to live in him.

But what does it look like to have a relationship with someone you can't see nor hear audibly?

And what can we do to grow and deepen that relationship?

Day 1

IN THE WOMB

As the Father has loved me, so have I loved you. Abide in my love.

John 15:9, esv

What does God want from you?

Some say *religion*. I don't. I think we can make a better case that Jesus came to destroy religion than to establish one.

Others say it's not religion; God wants *relationship*. I believe that is true. I just don't think it goes far enough.

One time Jesus said,

I am the vine; you are the branches. Whoever abides in me and I in him, he it is that bears much fruit, for apart from me you can do nothing. If anyone does not abide in me he is thrown away like a branch and withers; and the branches are gathered, thrown into the fire, and burned. If you abide in me, and my words abide in you, ask whatever you wish, and it will be done for you. By this my Father is glorified, that you bear much fruit and so prove to be my disciples.

As the Father has loved me, so have I loved you. Abide in my love.*

To "abide" means to live within. Jesus says he wants me to live inside him, and that he will live inside me. That sounds like more than a relationship to me.

Let's say you interviewed a baby inside his mother's womb and asked, "Do you have a relationship with your mother?"

I'm pretty sure the baby would give you a confused look. Babies in wombs look kind of like aliens, so you might not realize the baby looked confused, but he would.

The baby would say, "That's a clown question, bro." (I'm assuming babies in wombs can speak and are fully capable of making witty pop culture references.) The baby would continue, "Yes, we have a relationship, but it's much more than that. You may have noticed that *I live inside her*. You may not get it, but I actually *can't live without her*. I am *completely dependent on her* for everything that keeps me alive. Do you think I surround myself with her amniotic fluid to attract the babes?" (I'm assuming this baby is a boy, is already thinking about the opposite sex, and, to be ironic, calls the girls in other wombs "babes.")

"So, yes," the baby would say, "we *do* have a relationship, but just calling it a relationship seems to be a colossal understatement." (I'm assuming this baby uses cool words like *colossal*.)

"The next time you interview a baby in a womb," the baby would conclude, "you should ask more sensible questions. Now you'll have to excuse me; *The Maury Povich Show* is about to come back on and the paternity tests are in." (I'm assuming there are little TVs in moms' bellies and that babies like to watch Maury Povich because he often reveals the identity of the real father.)

If you were to ask God if what he really wants is a relationship with you, I can imagine him saying, "That's a clown question,

---

* John 15:5-9, ESV.

bro. I mean, yes, I guess it is a relationship, but did you catch the part where I said I want us to live inside each other? Call it what you want, but what I'm inviting you into is *much* more than a relationship. I'm offering to be the womb you exist within, and the blood that flows through your veins. I want to be the umbilical cord that brings you the fluids that sustain you, and I want to be those fluids that sustain you. What I want is for you to get lost inside of me, and I want to be lost inside of you. My desire is for us to be *one*. Now, if you'll excuse me, I have to go; *Happy Days* is on." (I'm assuming there's a big TV in heaven and that God likes to watch *Happy Days*.)

What God was describing before he started watching TV, that's what we need. Relationships are nice, but they're off and on; we move in and out of them. We need something deeper with God, something more constant.

We need that because we were made for it. Without it, we have a sense of emptiness.

We also need it because it's the only way we can live the life we were meant to live. Remember, we were meant to be like Jesus, to live holy lives. We would be incapable of that on our own, but we have God living inside us (and at the same time, we get to live inside him). God's abiding in us is what allows us to live like him.

God has offered to abide in us. We need to make sure we're abiding in him. Jesus didn't say, "As you abide in me." He said, "If you abide in me." We have a choice. And he told us to make the right one: "Abide in my love."

What would it look like to abide in Jesus?

I think it's about:

Getting other things out of the way, so I can let God have his way in me.

Pouring my heart out to God and letting God pour his love into me.

Trusting that if I have Jesus and nothing else, I have everything I need.

Giving top priority to God instead of to the preponderance of other things.

Giving up control and giving God control.

Tomorrow we'll think more about how we can get to that place.

•   •   •

Now What?

> Read Matthew 11:28-29.

> God invites us to come to him so we can lay down our burdens and rest. What burdens are weighing you down?

> What would it look like for you to give those burdens to God in prayer? Try it.

Day 2

GOD STALKERS

Whom have I in heaven but you? I desire you more than anything on earth.

PSALM 73:25

I WANT TO ENCOURAGE YOU TO BECOME A STALKER.

That may sound odd, because we've all heard scary stories of people like John Hinkley Jr., who because of his obsession stalked the actress Jodie Foster and then tried to assassinate President Ronald Reagan to impress her.*

There are other stories that are scary—and weird. Cristin Keleher became obsessed with former Beatle George Harrison, broke into his home, and while waiting for him, made herself a frozen pizza.**

William Lepeska was so desperate to see tennis star Anna Kournikova that he swam across the Biscayne Bay to get to her house. Unfortunately, he went to the wrong house. He was arrested at . . . the wrong house.***

---

* Because we all know that's how you impress the ladies.
** The weirdest part to me is the thought of an ex-Beatle purchasing or eating a frozen pizza.
*** If you're gonna swim across a large body of water, at least know the address. C'mon, that's just Stalking 101.

There are scary types of stalking, but there's also a less danger-ous variety. I'm thinking of a thirteen-year-old girl who becomes obsessed with a boy at school. She thinks about him all the time. She writes his name all over her notebooks. He may not know she exists, but she's got their babies' names picked out already.

She times her entire day—how she gets to her classes, when she goes to the bathroom—so she can see him as many times as possible. When she sees him she's like, "Ooooh, there he is! Oh, he's perfect! He takes my breath away! How will I live through this weekend without seeing him till Monday? I wonder what he's doing on Saturday? Maybe I could find out and somehow catch a glimpse of him on Saturday. He just looked my way! Did he notice me? What if . . . what if he were to come up to me? What if he were to talk to me?" This girl is obsessed with this guy, can't stop thinking about him, has to see him, and feels like she can't live without him. And so she stalks him.

God Stalker

A lot of people want God in their lives. Most people want God's blessings. But what we need to want is God himself.

A God stalker is someone who seeks God more than anything, who wants more and more of him, who realizes God is what he or she needs and goes after him. A God stalker is not someone who achieves "super Christian" status. *Every* Christian should be a God stalker, according to what God tells us. For instance, "'If you look for me wholeheartedly, you will find me. I will be found by you,' says the LORD,"* and "You must love the LORD your God with all your heart, all your soul, all your mind, and all your strength."**

Maybe the best example of a God stalker in the Bible is a guy from the Old Testament named David. He was the one who took on

---

* Jeremiah 29:13-14.
** Mark 12:30.

Goliath and later became king. David was a God stalker. He wasn't perfect. He messed up and sinned just like we do, but he knew God is the greatest treasure, so he'd get up and keep pursuing him.

Check out a love poem David wrote about God:

O God, you are my God;
    I earnestly search for you.
My soul thirsts for you;
    my whole body longs for you
in this parched and weary land
    where there is no water.
I have seen you in your sanctuary
    and gazed upon your power and glory.
Your unfailing love is better than life itself;
    how I praise you!
I will praise you as long as I live,
    lifting up my hands to you in prayer.
You satisfy me more than the richest feast.
    I will praise you with songs of joy.

I lie awake thinking of you,
    meditating on you through the night.
Because you are my helper,
    I sing for joy in the shadow of your wings.
I cling to you;
    your strong right hand holds me securely.*

See what I mean?

Christians often talk about having a friendship with God, and it is true that God offers us friendship. But I've got lots of friends, and I don't talk to any of them this way! I've never gone up to a

---

* Psalm 63:1-8.

friend and said, "Dude, earnestly I seek you; my soul thirsts for you. Because you are glorious. In fact, last night when I was in bed thinking of you, I just started to sing . . ."

This isn't friendship language; this is stalker language. And it doesn't end there. David also wrote, "Come quickly, LORD, and answer me, for my depression deepens. Don't turn away from me, or I will die."* He sounds like that middle-school girl: "I am so depressed! If I don't see him soon, I . . . am . . . going . . . to . . . die!"

Do you see why I call David a God stalker? And God called David "a man after my own heart."**

That's what I want for me and for you.

Here's the good news: God isn't avoiding us. In fact, God promises to be with us all the time.*** So we don't need to go out searching for him; we just need to pay attention. People have called this "practicing the presence of God." We remember he's with us, train our minds on him, and seek to stay in constant contact.

How? I love the advice Max Lucado gives in his book *Just Like Jesus*. He suggests that you first give God your *waking* thoughts. When you wake in the morning, focus your initial thoughts on him. Then give God your *waiting* thoughts. Spend some quiet time with God, sharing your heart with him and listening for his voice. Third, give God your *whispering* thoughts. Repeatedly offer up brief prayers throughout the day. You might repeat the same short prayer: "God, am I pleasing you?" "Am I in your will, Lord?" "I love and want to follow you, Jesus." Then last, give God your *waning* thoughts. Talk to God as you're falling asleep. Review your day with him. End your day by telling him you love him.

That's something you can do.

You can go after God's heart.

You can be a God stalker.

---

* Psalm 143:7.
** Acts 13:22.
*** See, for instance, John 14:16-17 and Matthew 28:20.

• • •

Now What?

> Read Matthew 13:44-46.

> Jesus is saying that if you had to give away everything to have God in your life, it would be the best trade you'd ever make. What have you had to give up to have God in your life? What might you? What would be hardest to give up? Why do you think God is worth giving up everything for?

> Generally we want to pray from our hearts with our own words. But some people find value at times in praying a prayer written by someone else. People have especially done this with the Psalms in the Bible. Today, pray Psalm 63:1-8 or Psalm 40, making the words your own and praying them from your heart.

Day 3

LAY YOUR HEAD IN HIS LAP

Pray in the Spirit at all times and on every occasion. Stay alert and

be persistent in your prayers for all believers everywhere.

EPHESIANS 6:18

SPEAKER AND AUTHOR BRENNAN MANNING used to tell a story about a woman who asked a priest to come speak to her father, who was on his deathbed. The priest agreed to come right over.

The daughter let the priest in and told him her father was in his bedroom. When the priest walked in, he noticed an empty chair next to the bed. He said, "I see you're expecting me."

The man in the bed said, "No. Who are you?" The priest explained that the daughter had invited him to come over and talk to her father about God.

The man nodded and said, "I have a question for you." He explained that he had always believed in God and Jesus, but never knew how to pray. One time he asked a preacher at church, who gave him a book to read. On the first page there were two or three words he didn't know. He gave up reading after a few pages and continued not to pray.

A few years later he was at work talking to a Christian friend named Joe. He mentioned to Joe that he didn't know how to pray. Joe seemed confused. He said, "Are you kidding? Well, here's what you do. Take an empty chair, put it next to you. Picture Jesus sitting in that chair, and talk to him. Tell him how you feel about him, tell him about your life, tell him about your needs."

The man gestured to the empty chair next to his bed and said, "I've been doing that for years. Is that wrong?"

"No." The priest smiled. "That's great. You just keep doing that." The two of them talked a little longer, and then the priest left.

About a week later the man's daughter called the priest. She explained, "I just wanted to let you know that my father died yesterday. Thanks again for visiting him; he enjoyed talking to you."

The priest said, "I hope he died peacefully."

"Well, it was interesting," the daughter told him. "I had to go to the store yesterday, so I went in my dad's bedroom. He was fine. He made a corny joke, and I left. When I came back he was dead. But here's the strange part: right before he died he crawled out of bed, and he died with his head lying on that empty chair."

Prayer Is

Relationships are all about love and are based on communication. What God is looking for is relationship, not religion. If we're going to have a real relationship with God, it's going to be about love and based on communication.

Prayer is communicating with God. But it's more than that. Prayer is love. God loves us, and his love calls for us to respond. Prayer comes not from gritting your teeth and engaging in a "discipline"; prayer comes from falling in love. Prayer is shared intimacy with God. Prayer is putting your head in your loving Father's lap.

On one hand, prayer is as simple as that. You don't need to read a book with big words; you just need to pull up an empty chair. You don't need a bunch of seminars; you just need an open heart.

On the other hand, prayer is an unnatural activity in some ways. It's talking to God, but we're not used to talking to someone we can't see. It's letting God speak to us, but we're not used to listening to someone we can't audibly hear. I don't want to make prayer more complicated than it is, but if you're new to prayer or struggle with prayer, it can be a bit confusing. So let me share a few thoughts that have helped my prayer life.

Growing in Prayer

Prayer isn't just a part of our day; it should be the air we breathe. The Bible says, "pray continually"* and "on all occasions."** Prayer is sharing our lives, our thoughts, and our moments with God, so it's something that we can and should do all the time.

However, we need to take some special time to devote to prayer each day. Why? Because fixing our focus on God will help us to keep our focus on him the rest of the day. Because we'll go deeper in that special quiet time than we will in the hustle and bustle of the rest of the day. It's the same as in a marriage. My wife and I might spend a whole day together and kind of talk about a thousand things, but until we stop doing something else and sit down and look at each other, we probably won't talk about anything of substance.

When should you do that prayer time? Well, it's the most important part of your day, so you should give it the best time of your day. Are you a morning person? Then spend time with God when you first wake up. Or does your brain not start functioning till after twelve cups of coffee? Then maybe lunchtime would be a better choice. Some people prefer to devote the last part of their day to focusing on God in prayer.

And you can be creative in that time. Sometimes I think my prayers. Other times I talk out loud.*** More often, I write my prayers

---

* 1 Thessalonians 5:17, NIV.
** Ephesians 6:18, NIV.
*** If you're going to pray out loud, you should be alone! Otherwise your prayers could lead to your being institutionalized.

in a journal.* I've also gone on prayer walks. And I've been known to put on some worship music and spend some of my time with God, singing to him. What's important is love; that we're really connecting with God.

Experiment and see what helps you to really connect with God.

And if none of those ways work, you can always just pull up an empty chair.

•   •   •

Now What?

> Read Matthew 6:5-13.

> Jesus gives us a model, or an outline, for prayer, not the exact words we're to pray. Our words shouldn't be recited but should come from our hearts. Read through Jesus' model prayer again. What types of things is he saying we should pray about?

> Use Jesus' model prayer in Matthew 6:9-13 as an outline for your prayers today. Prayerfully read an idea, like "Father in heaven, hallowed be your name" (NIV), and then take a moment to continue praying that idea in your own words.

---

* I've got ADD issues, and writing helps me to stay focused instead of trying to pray and then finding my mind wandering to where I should take my wife on our date that week. Speaking of dates, I just heard about this restaurant that makes amazing date milk shakes. Speaking of milk shakes, one time my son asked me my favorite food, and I said, "Well, I guess milk shakes," and he laughed and said, "Milk shakes are not food." But I told him of course they're food. Speaking of food, I need to hit the grocery store . . . Wait, what was I writing about? ADD strikes again.

Day 4

FED FOR A LIFETIME

You have been believers so long now that you ought to be teaching others.
Instead, you need someone to teach you again the basic things about God's
word. You are like babies who need milk and cannot eat solid food.

Hebrews 5:12

WHEN I HAD THE IDEA, I didn't picture a burly Navy SEAL sitting in my lap, but that's the way it turned out. And you know what they say: "When life gives you a Navy SEAL, feed him like a little baby."*

It seems like there are people in every church who complain, "I'm not getting fed in this church." I have a friend who replies, "There are only two kinds of people who can't feed themselves—imbeciles and infants. Which one are you?" Pretty harsh, but he makes a point. Pretty quickly, children learn how to feed themselves food, and Christians should learn how to feed themselves spiritually.

That was the point I was making with the Navy SEAL. I was preaching a sermon, and I started with a baby in my arms and fed

---

* I may have just made that up.

him. Everyone made "Oh, that's adorable" faces, and "That baby is so cute in our pastor's arms" noises. I gave the baby back to his mother and launched into a message on the importance of reading the Bible every day. I told everyone, "Give a man a fish, feed him for a day. Teach a man to fish, feed him for a lifetime."* I ended the message by trying to illustrate how wrong it is for people who are no longer spiritual infants to rely on someone else to feed them. I asked for a volunteer and Mr. Navy SEAL raised his hand. The church I pastored in Virginia Beach had a bunch of SEALs, but it hadn't occurred to me that one would volunteer. He came up, and I asked him to sit in my lap. I had a jar of baby food, and I asked him if I could feed him. And everyone made "Oh, that's disturbing" faces, and "That muscular man is so awkward in our pastor's arms" noises.

Is It That Important?

Is it really that important to read the Bible on your own? Yes, it is.

If you go to church weekly, isn't hearing the sermon enough Bible? No, it isn't.

It's *critical* that we read and study and know and apply the Bible. Why?

- Because we love God and want to experience his love more and more. The Bible is like a letter God wrote to us. Can you imagine receiving love letters from someone and never opening them? The Bible says God is love, and we grow in his love as we read what he's written to us.

- The Bible also gives us guidance in life. It's so easy to feel lost or to lose direction. God gave us wisdom in the Bible that provides the direction we need.

---

* Just made that up too. (At leat, I wish I had!)

- It's also important to read the Bible consistently because it helps us know what's true and what's not.

Studying the Bible is key to spiritual maturity. If you don't get into God's Word, I'm not sure you can grow much spiritually.

What Do I Do?

The Bible is a big book. Where do you start, and how do you read it?

I've always preferred reading through whole books of the Bible. Some people hunt and peck, but when you go through a book of the Bible you're getting the whole context of what you're reading. You understand who wrote it, whom it was written to, what issues are being addressed.

I also suggest reading the New Testament before the Old. The Old Testament comes first chronologically, but it's more challenging to understand because it describes a time more distant from us. When we know the New Testament it helps us to understand the Old. And the New Testament is where we meet Jesus, and it's all about Jesus.

Before I read, I ask God to speak to me through his Word. I want to read the Bible with a humble spirit and get everything I can out of it.

As I read, I ask three questions.

First, *Say what?* My problem is that I tend to be in a hurry and can read a chapter of the Bible, then have no idea what I just read. But the Bible is too important for me to skim over. So I slow myself down by asking some "Say what?" questions like "What did it say?" and "What did I learn about God?" and "What did I learn about myself?"

Second, *So what?* Imagine someone read the same Bible passage you just did, then asked you, "So what? What does this have to do with life today?" What would you answer? What's the life principle in the passage?

113

Sometimes this is easy. You read a verse that says, "Do not judge." What does that mean for today? It means do not judge. Other times it's not so easy. For instance, there's a verse in the Bible that says not to eat meat that's been sacrificed to idols.* Um, I don't think they sell that kind of meat at my grocery store, so can I skip that verse? Actually, no, you can't. With a look at the context and a little digging, you'd discover that in the early days of Christianity there was a debate between two groups. One thought nothing of buying and eating meat that had been sacrificed to the god of another religion. The other felt that doing so was the equivalent of participating in that other religion. The issue was taken to the church leaders, who finally laid down a verdict. They basically said, "Meat that's been offered to idols is no different than what they put in a Quarter Pounder with Cheese. Why? Because idols aren't real; they just represent false gods. So it doesn't offend God that you eat meat that's been sacrificed to them. *But* it does offend some people. By eating that meat you are causing them to stumble in their spiritual walk. So just don't eat it. Be willing to give up your freedom to help others."

So is there a principle in "Don't eat meat sacrificed to idols"? Absolutely. And that leads to the last question I ask when I read the Bible.

Third, *Now what?* This goes beyond the universal lesson to *your* specific application. How should your life be changed based on what you read? With that verse about not eating meat sacrificed to idols, maybe you feel like it's okay for you to have a glass of wine with a meal, but you're having dinner with a friend who's a recovering alcoholic. This verse would say that you don't have a drink, because it might cause him to stumble. Or perhaps you have a revealing bathing suit you like to wear sunbathing in the backyard, but you're going to a pool party with a bunch of guys. This verse

---

* Acts 15:20.

would say that you don't wear the bathing suit, because you know guys tend to have a problem with lust. The *Now what?* question helps us to apply what we've read, and obeying God by applying the Bible is the key to loving God* and being blessed by him.**

If you have a Bible, you can feed yourself, and if you do, your life will be changed.

Or . . . I can call you up on stage and shove a spoon of baby food in your mouth, but trust me, you wouldn't like that.

●　　●　　●

Now What?

> ➤ Read James 1:22-25.

> ➤ *Say what?* What does this passage say about not just reading but applying the Bible to your life? *So what?* Why do you think applying the Bible is so essential in truly living for God? *Now what?* What could help you to be more consistent in looking for the "Now What?" and applying it to your life?

> ➤ Yesterday you read the story of the guy who prayed by pulling up a chair and picturing Jesus sitting in it. Why don't you try that today? Picture Jesus sitting next to you and talk to him as if he were your best friend (because he is).

---

* See John 14:15.
** See James 1:25.

Day 5

WHERE YOUR HEART IS

Don't store up treasures here on earth, where moths eat them and rust destroys

them, and where thieves break in and steal. Store your treasures in heaven,

where moths and rust cannot destroy, and thieves do not break in and steal.

Wherever your treasure is, there the desires of your heart will also be.

MATTHEW 6:19-21

SINCE HAVING KIDS, my wife and I don't exchange Christmas presents. I'm just too cheap. But before she gave birth to the fruit of my loins, we used to each have a budget of $100 to spend on each other for Christmas. One year Jen told me she wanted a diamond tennis bracelet. I went to the store and the clerk showed me the diamond tennis bracelet I could get for $100. I stared at it and asked, "Are you sure those are diamonds? It looks more like little pieces of . . . glitter."

I bought it and gave it to Jen on Christmas morning. She exclaimed, "Just what I wanted, a glitter tennis bracelet!"

A few days later the clasp on it broke. I wasn't surprised. I took it back in to get fixed. The day before, Jen's grandma had given each of us $100. It was her annual present, and the only money we each had every year to splurge on ourselves. As I waited for the clasp to be fixed, I noticed the $200 tennis bracelets. You could actually see the diamonds!

A few hours later I handed Jen her tennis bracelet. She looked at it and asked, "Wait? Did the glitter grow?"

I smiled, "Actually, I got you a better one."

She was confused. "Where did you get the money? Wait, you used my grandma's money, didn't you? Why? What . . . what made you do this?"

I told her the truth. "Love made me do it."

All Kinds of Reasons

I want you to think about giving. Like giving . . . money . . . to God, through the church. People don't like to hear about giving, but God talks about it—a lot. In fact, check out the number of times these important words appear in the Bible:

Believe: 272 times

Pray: 374 times

Love: 714 times

Give: 2,162 times*

And that's just the word *give*. Often the word you'll see in the Bible is *tithe*. The word *tithe* means "tenth"; to tithe is to give God the first tenth of whatever you bring in. You'll also see the word *offering*. An offering is anything you give to God *above* ten percent.

We're to give generously to God, and there are all kinds of reasons to do so. For instance:

It's God's money, not ours. We think of it as our money, but God says it's his.** The only reason we have money is because he's given us the ability to earn it. So really, we're not giving God some of our

---

* These numbers may vary a little bit from one translation to another, but you get the idea.
** For instance, see Psalm 24:1 and 1 Corinthians 4:2.

money; God lets us keep most of his money, and we give him back a little bit of it.

God has commanded us to give money back to him. All through the Old Testament he commands people to give him ten percent.* In the New Testament he sends his Son Jesus** to live and die for us, and then he commands us to give generously.*** All along people had great reasons to give generously back to God, but now we have a *much* greater reason.

*God will bless us for tithing.**** If I have a choice of God's blessings or ten percent of my money, I'm taking God's blessings every day!

Giving increases our faith. It helps us to trust in God more and in ourselves less. It's scary at first deciding to live off of only ninety percent of our incomes, but not only does it demonstrate faith, it grows our faith as we see how God provides for us.

Tithing helps set our priorities. God tells us that we're to give him the *first* ten percent.***** Not our leftovers, but the first check we write. When we do that, it helps to clarify that God is most important in our lives.

Giving to God allows us to have an eternal impact with our money. We have lots of choices for how to spend our money. Most of what we spend it on ends up in a toilet or a trash dump. What we give to God through the church goes toward his mission of bringing his lost children home to him and to an eternity in heaven. *That* is what I want to spend my money on!

The Love Reason

There are all kinds of reasons to give generously back to God, but right now I just want you to focus on one. One I haven't mentioned

---

* See, for instance, Leviticus 27:30.
** Jesus, by the way, affirmed tithing. See Luke 11:42 and Matthew 23:23.
*** 2 Corinthians 9 is one example of this.
**** For instance, see Deuteronomy 12:6-7; Malachi 3:10-12; and 2 Corinthians 9:6.
***** See, for instance, Proverbs 3:9 and Deuteronomy 18:4.

yet: love. Giving expresses my love for God, it helps me experience God's love for me, and it grows my love for God.

That may sound odd to you, but it's straight from Jesus.

He says, "Those who accept my commandments and obey them are the ones who love me. And because they love me, my Father will love them. And I will love them and reveal myself to each of them."* We've been commanded to be generous toward God with our money. Those who love Jesus will "accept" and "obey" that command. And because they love God in that way, God's love will be revealed to them. Those who do it experience God's love.

Jesus also says, "Wherever your treasure is, there the desires of your heart will also be."** In other words, you put your money into what you care about, and you care about what you put your money into.

Isn't it true that you put your money into what you care about? In fact, I could know a ton about you by looking at your checkbook and your credit card statement.

And isn't it also true that when you put money into something, you start to care about it more? Like if you have an old clunker car, you don't care about it. If you pick up your friend and he has some food and asks, "Can I eat in your car?" you'd laugh and say, "Eat in it? You can butcher cows in it for all I care." But if you go out and spend some serious money on a new car you would tell your friend, "No, you can't eat in my car! In fact, I don't want you to even breathe in my car!" When your money goes to God, you begin to care more and more about him.

The inverse is true too. If we care so much about our money that we won't give it, then we lose a significant opportunity to connect with God and grow. In fact, it moves us in the opposite direction from God. Jesus says, "No one can serve two masters. Either you

---

* John 14:21.
** Matthew 6:21.

will hate one and love the other, or you will be devoted to one and despise the other. You cannot serve both God and money."* The Bible even says that the love of money can pull us away from our faith. "For the love of money is the root of all kinds of evil. And some people, craving money, have wandered from the true faith and pierced themselves with many sorrows."**

Give generously back to God. Don't try to figure out the minimum you have to give him; see how *much* you can give him. You will be so glad you did. Other people might think you're crazy, but when they look at you funny and ask why, just smile and say, "Love made me do it."

• • •

Now What?

➤ Read 2 Corinthians 9:1-15.

➤ What do you learn about giving from this passage? Take some time to create a plan for giving. How much will you give God? What is generous? When and how will you increase your giving?

➤ Money often provides the most competition with God for our worship, and it is often the last thing people will really give to God. Take some time to pray about your finances. Ask God to reveal your heart to you and where it needs to change when it comes to money. Ask him to help you make him a higher priority than money and what you can buy with it.

---

* Luke 16:13, NIV.
** 1 Timothy 6:10.

Community

We were created in the image of God.
And God lives in community.

We were designed to live in community.
We were not meant to do life alone. And
we can't do our Christian lives alone.

That's why God puts people into a
spiritual family we call "church."

But it may seem easier to just fly solo. Why do
we need the church? And what is the church
supposed to be like? What is it supposed to do?

Let's take a look at all this. And, for fun, let's look
at it through the lens of some blockbuster movies.

Day 1

NOT GOOD

It is not good for the man to be alone.

GENESIS 2:18

IN *CAST AWAY*, Tom Hanks plays a successful FedEx executive who is on a flight that unexpectedly goes down over the ocean.* Tom is the only survivor of the crash,** and he ends up on a deserted island.*** He spends four isolated years on this island. His only friend is a volleyball with a bloody face drawn on it. Tom becomes very attached to it, but it's not really a great companion. I mean, you wouldn't want to take it to the prom or anything like that.

Tom tries to adjust and build a happy life for himself on the island. After all, his mama always told him, life is like a box of

---

* Now that I think about it, I suppose every flight that goes down is unexpected. I doubt any flight manifest ever included the line, "3:00: Crash over the Pacific."
** Tom also survived, against the odds, in *Apollo 13* and in *Captain Phillips*. And his career survived the TV show *Bosom Buddies* and the movie *Joe Versus the Volcano*. So I think today's lesson is: Tom Hanks is amazing at surviving!
*** I'm just now realizing I don't really understand the term "deserted island." Is the island deserted *before* someone washes up on it? Or does it need a person stranded there to be deserted? But wouldn't someone have to *leave* the island for it to technically be deserted? When a person washes up, we call the island deserted, but didn't it actually just *stop* being deserted?

chocolates, you never know what you're going to get. But he finds that task impossible.

You know how movies will sometimes have subtitles? Like *Rambo 17: The Final Fury*, or *Dumb and Dumber To: We Should Have Stuck with Just One*. Well, I think this Tom Hanks movie should have been titled *Cast Away: It Is Not Good for Man to Be Alone*.

Alone

The Bible begins with God creating, and it's clear that he's enjoying the process. In fact, each time God creates, he celebrates with a bit of a touchdown dance. God creates light, land, and water, and for each thing God creates, he takes a moment to declare that it is good. It's almost as if he gives himself a congratulatory high five.

Then God gets to the pinnacle of his creative genius. He creates a man named Adam. But for the first time, God pauses and says, "There's something not good here." Weird. But God specifically diagnoses the problem. "It is not good for man to be alone." That's the line. That's the movie *Cast Away*. And in that moment, God makes a radical statement about the essential nature of human relationships.

What's crazy about God's statement is the timing. Soon something happens that theologians call the Fall. Man sins against God. That rebellion severs man's ability to do life with God. Sin comes in like a cancer and starts infecting everything.

But that's later. Before the Fall, man is able to live in perfect relationship with God. That's why it's odd that God says Adam is alone and describes his condition as "not good."

Some say that every person has a God-shaped hole inside that only God can fill. I believe that. I tell people that. But what we seem to learn in Genesis is that every human being also has a people-shaped hole that only people can fill. A hole that even God can't fill.* That's why someone can have a perfect relationship with God and still be called "alone" and in a situation that is "not good."

You need God. But you also need people. And all the success in the world, all the fame, all the money and possessions cannot replace your need for people.

You were made for community with God and with people. I'm talking about a need that only a deep connectedness will meet. You can live in a busy city surrounded by neighbors, have hundreds of coworkers, and even show up every Sunday to a church full of people but still live out your own *Cast Away* kind of story.

We need deep relationships, because it is not good for humans to be alone. We weren't meant to live alone. We were created in the image of God, and God lives in community. If we're isolated, we are defying our very design. And we will struggle.

The Struggle

We struggle when we are alone, because people don't grow well in isolation.

It's so easy to lie to ourselves. We hear the advice that we need to just "follow our hearts," but God warns us that our hearts are deceitful.** For instance, I can read the Bible and hypothetically agree with it, but in reality not be applying what I read. But when I have other people who know and love me, they can speak truth into my life, truth I need to hear.

We will also struggle when we are alone, because people don't recover well in isolation.

There are ups and downs in the Christian life. Well, there are ups and downs in life, and Christians aren't exempt. I've had my fair share of the roller-coaster ride. What I've noticed is that typically things are on a pretty even keel. The highs and lows generally don't last long. But I've had two prolonged seasons in the valley. When I

---

* Nor, for that matter, can a volleyball fill it. (Sorry, Wilson.)
** See Jeremiah 17:9.

look back and try to discern what was different, why I wasn't able to bounce back, I realize . . . I was isolated.

The Bible says, "Two people are better off than one, for they can help each other succeed. If one person falls, the other can reach out and help. But someone who falls alone is in real trouble."* You can't do life alone because when you do, you'll find that you can't get up.** When you experience what's been called the "dark night of the soul," you need someone who knows you deeply and who cares enough to talk sense to you, encourage you, and pull you out.

All of this is why "God places the lonely in families."*** His desire is for every isolated person to find a community of love and support. And because he loves us, God designed that kind of community for us. We call it church.

People will sometimes talk negatively about church today. Some say they don't need church.

While it is true that no church is perfect, and there are some black eyes in the church's history, the truth is that most churches are a lot closer to God's design than they're given credit for.

And the truth is that we need church.

Just ask Tom Hanks.

•   •   •

Now What?

> Read Acts 2:42-47 and Acts 4:32-35.

> This was a long time ago, so in some ways these people's lives were very different from ours. However, despite

---

* Ecclesiastes 4:9-10.
** Yes, you will be like those old ladies in the commercials who are lying on the bathroom floor yelling for help, but no one comes. Don't be that old lady!
*** Psalm 68:6.

the fact that it may look a little different, we can still have that kind of community in our lives. And that's the question: Do you have this kind of community in your life? If not, what would be the best way for you to get it? How do you think it would benefit your life? What initiative would you need to take? Take it! If you do have that kind of community, is there anyone who might be alone whom you could invite into your community?

➤ How about today you pray with someone else? Or, if it's not possible today, at least schedule a time when you can pray with someone else. It might be with your spouse, your child, a fellow Christian at your job, or someone from your church. You can use this book as an excuse—tell them it's an assignment you have to do. When you pray with the other person, don't try to sound super spiritual. Just talk to God like you always do.

Day 2

A COMMUNITY OF GRACE

Upon this rock I will build my church, and all the

powers of hell will not conquer it.

MATTHEW 16:18

THE MOVIE *LONE SURVIVOR* is the true story of some guys who decide they want to become Navy SEALs. They go into training as tough "I don't need anyone but me" individuals but soon realize they *do* need each other. The mission they've signed up for is so big and so challenging that they can't do it on their own. They need to link arms and become a community.

And that's exactly what happens. They become a united community.

It's a different kind of community than most people might ever experience.

Their community is unique in that it's a community on a mission. Typically, people join a group because it's good for them. Membership has its privileges. And if there aren't enough privileges, people don't want to be members.

But not the Navy SEALs. The SEALs aren't about serving themselves, but serving others. They are a community that exists to protect those who are not part of the community. They keep the mission first. To accomplish their mission, they have to support each other. We see this in the movie as four of the SEALs go into action in Afghanistan. Things don't go as planned, and as they face seemingly insurmountable odds, they constantly encourage each other.

Their community is also unique in that it's a community of grace.

Toward the beginning of their surveillance mission in Afghanistan, the four SEALs are in the woods, spying on the Taliban camp, when they're accidentally discovered by an elderly shepherd and two teenage goat herders. The SEALs realize that if they let these three civilians go, they will run and alert the Taliban to their presence. The Taliban will soon show up, and the SEALs will probably die.

The other option is to save themselves by killing the three civilians.

To most it would seem like an easy decision: save yourself! But it's not so obvious for these men. Ultimately they choose grace—to let the shepherds go, even though it may lead to their own deaths. And letting them go . . . goes badly. The shepherds run and alert the Taliban, who show up, guns blazing. Still, one of the Navy SEALs says, "I think we did the right thing. We let our love light shine."

In the battle, three of the four SEALs die.* And the lone survivor of this community of grace, Marcus Luttrell, ends up being saved by a different community of grace.

Marcus is severely injured. A local named Mohammed Gulab and his son come along and rescue him. They take Marcus to their village and care for him. When the Taliban come looking, Gulab risks his life, his family, and his entire village to protect Marcus. He explains to the Taliban that his tribe's tradition of hospitality requires them to protect Marcus at all costs.

So Marcus, who led his team in making the decision to be a

---

* It's not a spoiler. The movie is called *LONE* Survivor, not *Three out of Four Survivors*.

community of grace to the three shepherds, is now saved by a community of grace.

A Unique Community

Maybe you learned, as I did, to be an "I don't need anyone but me" individual. It sounds so good. Then life happens. And, well, some supportive friends might be nice.

Then we decide to follow Jesus. And the scope of our mission seems overwhelming, and the temptations and confusion assail us, and we realize that we can't do this on our own.

That's why we need the church. A lot of people say they can be Christians without being part of a church. Technically that may be true, but in the daily grind of real life it just doesn't work. We need one another, and God wants us to become part of a unified community. He wants us to link arms with a church. And the church is a different kind of community than many people have ever experienced.

Like we see with the SEALs in *Lone Survivor*, the church is unique in that it's a community on a mission.

A guy named William Temple once said, "The church is the only society that exists for the benefit of those who are not its members." Christians can treat the church like it's a purveyor of religious goods and services, and they are the customers, but, um, that's wrong. The church exists to love and serve and share truth and hope with those who don't yet belong. The goal is to bring people into God's family. Until people become God's children, the church exists for them. Once they do, it no longer does.

It may sound like Christians get the raw end of the deal on that one. We want things to be for us, to serve us. But once we start living life in the upside-down way of Jesus, we realize we've had it all wrong. Jesus was right; it is better to serve than to be served.* And

---

* See Mark 9:35 and 10:42-45.

becoming a part of a community on a mission fills our lives with purpose and adventure.

The church is also unique in that it's a community of grace.

There aren't many places dealing grace in this world. Seems like everywhere you go you're accepted based on your merits or rejected because you don't measure up.

Grace is giving someone better than they deserve. It's giving love even when the person may not deserve love. It's offering acceptance to people you may not be keen on accepting. The Bible says, "Accept each other just as Christ has accepted you."* How does Christ accept you?

He doesn't ask how much money you have or how intelligent you are.

He doesn't ask if you were voted most attractive or most likely to succeed.

He doesn't ask what kind of car you drive or how many square feet you live in.

He doesn't ask if you've been a good boy or girl.

No, Jesus' only question is, "Do you want my love?"

Jesus came to establish his church,** and his church is to be a community of grace where the only requirement is that you're willing to be loved—by God and by the other members of the community.

And that is exactly what you need. You need to get better than you deserve. Because we've all blown it. Because none of us are good enough if we're judged on our own merits.

You need to find and become part of a community of grace, and you need to start wholesaling grace—for free—to everyone you can.

(What are you waiting for?)

(Go do it.)

---

* Romans 15:7.
** See Matthew 16:18 and Ephesians 2:19-22.

• • •

Now What?

> Read Ephesians 4:1-16.

> How do you see the church being a community of grace and on a mission? Who has God put in your life or in your community whom you could show some grace to? Is there some way you could team up with other people from your church to show a ton of grace to some people who really need it?

> Ask God to help you see today the ways that you don't show grace to other people. Ask him to show you people who need to experience his grace through you.

Day 3

FREAKS ON A MISSION

[God] said, "My grace is all you need. My power works best
in weakness." So now I am glad to boast about my weaknesses,
so that the power of Christ can work through me.

2 Corinthians 12:9

The X-Men started out as a comic book in 1963. It's become one of the bestselling comic book series of all time and led to a popular movie series.

In the series, there's a "new evolution" happening in the world, and some humans are experiencing mutations. Not mutations like having twelve fingers but instead powers that allow the person to do amazing things.

The problem is that society views the mutants as different and scary, and so people shun and even persecute them.

Charles Xavier is a mistreated mutant, but he refuses to let bitterness overtake him. At one point another abused mutant friend of his says, "You know, Charles, I used to think it's gonna be you and me against the world. But no matter how bad the world gets, you don't wanna be against it, do you?" He doesn't. In fact, he decides to become "Dr. X," a force for good in the world. He invites another mutant, Erik Lensherr, to join him, saying, "You have a chance to become a part of something much bigger than yourself." But Lensherr refuses and becomes the villain Magneto.

Soon Dr. X starts what is, allegedly, a school for gifted kids but is actually a refuge for mutants. Many of them have been hurt or disowned by their parents because they're different, but at this safe haven they find love and healing. Dr. X also trains them to use their mutant abilities as weapons, to try to save the world from the evil that Magneto is seeking to unleash on it.

Fiction?

I'll be honest with you: I'm not an X-Men movies kind of guy. I won't tell you the kinds of movies I prefer,* but I think the issue I have with superhero movies is that they seem so unrealistic. Still, there's something oddly realistic about the X-Men.

Now, to buy my premise, you're going to have to agree that we're mutants. I don't mean that there's a new evolution happening or that you're growing unusual body parts. I mean that we're all strange in our own way. We have quirks, bad habits, hang-ups, and painful experiences that have left scars. We're not quite right. We're mutants.

In fact, it may be freeing for you to say it out loud. Try it, loud and proud: "I am a mutant."**

What makes you feel different or like you aren't what you're "supposed to be"? Maybe everyone around you is either getting married or is already married, but you're still single or are divorced. Or perhaps others seem happy and have everything going for them, but you are struggling with an addiction or depression. Or it could

---

* But I will say they're the type where high schoolers play basketball in the Indiana state tournament and someone shouts, "Hickory!" in an empty gym and the underdog team ends up winning in the end. Or the type where some undersized kid works to make the big-time college football team and everyone in the stands chants his name so he finally gets in the game and ends up being carried off the field. Just, generally, those kinds of movies.
** I don't suggest you do this if you're on some form of public transportation. Other people might look at you funny.

be that you were abused as a child, and it's left you feeling damaged. You feel like you're not quite right. You're a mutant. So am I.

What does the world do with mutants? As in the film, the world tends to shun and sometimes persecute those who are different or not good enough in some way. So like the mutants in the movie, we tend to live in fear and keep what makes us different a secret.

So what should we do? Where do we turn?

To the church.

God's Way

God has always had a thing for choosing people who aren't exactly perfect specimens with picture-perfect pasts.

God chose Joseph to save God's people from famine, despite the fact that Joseph came from a family so dysfunctional that his brothers sold him into slavery.

He chose Gideon, a fear-driven wimp, to lead his army.

God chose Ruth to be one of Jesus' ancestors, even though Ruth was childless, a widow, and a foreigner.

God chose Moses to represent him and be his spokesperson—an unexpected choice, since Moses had a serious stuttering problem.

Oh, and did I mention that Moses was a murderer? God even chooses people whose "mutations" are a result of their own sins and bad choices.

God chose Abraham to be the father of faith, even though Abraham had a serious problem with lying.

God chose to save Noah from the Flood. You might think, "Well, Noah must have been perfect." Actually, after the Flood, Noah got drunk and passed out completely naked.

God chose Rahab for a starring role in the Bible. She was a prostitute.

He chose David, an adulterer, to be the leader of his people.

I could go on and on. God chooses messy people with problems.

And that makes me feel really good, because this means God would choose me. And God created the church to be a safe haven for these mutants, to be a place of love for those who might seem a bit defective.

But not only is the church a place of acceptance, it's also a training center for people who want to learn to use their abilities to become part of a team with the mission of saving the world. And here's the crazy part: it's not only your best skills and traits that can be used in that mission. God wants to redeem your "mutantness" and use it to love the world and draw people to him. We see God do this all through the Bible, and he wants to do it in you.

So how might God use your weakness as a strength in his love revolution?

Maybe you were divorced, but will find healing, and God will use you to minister to others going through a divorce.

Perhaps you've struggled with an addiction. But God has or is going to lead you through recovery and then hold you up to some of your friends as an example of how he can bring supernatural healing to a person's life.

If you suffer with depression, God may take it away from you, but maybe he won't. It could be that God won't completely take it away, but he'll still make you a different person. You will have an underlying joy that people can see, even with your depression, and people will notice that difference, and they'll turn to God because of it.

God wants to use you as a superhero in saving the world. One of the cool things about X-Men that makes it unique from most superhero stories is that the X-Men are a team of superheroes.* And that's what the church is!

Each of us has our redeemed mutant qualities, and the Bible tells us that each of us also has special abilities (the Bible refers

---

* Think about it: if Superman goes on vacation or pulls a hamstring, we're all toast!

to them as "spiritual gifts") to offer, like the ability to encourage people, teach, lead, or show mercy. They may be simple abilities, but when God empowers them, they become kind of superhero powers, and we become capable of doing things we could never do on our own, to help God in his mission of love. But we can't do it alone, which is why God puts us on a team. God joins us together, and with his power we become a team that can truly turn the world upside down.

•   •   •

Now What?

> Read 1 Corinthians 12:1-31.

> Where do you currently serve in your church? If you're not volunteering, start. God's plan is for every follower of Jesus to play an important role in the church. If you are serving, do you feel like your volunteer position is a good fit for you? If not, maybe talk to a pastor in your church about finding a new role where you can make a bigger impact.

> God put you in this world not to live for yourself, but to live for him and to serve others. Ask God to make you the kind of person who can make the biggest impact for him that you can.

Day 4

EVERYTHING IS AWESOME?

If the Son sets you free, you are truly free.

John 8:36

In *The LEGO Movie*, President Business rules over the LEGO world. He wants everyone to follow the instructions. He enforces the rules and threatens anyone who doesn't behave. His goal is conformity. President Business is all about the externals. He wants everyone to agree that "everything is awesome" and to look good and look happy, even if they're not.

Emmett is your average, ordinary, everyday LEGO guy. He starts every day by reading the instructions on how to "fit in, have everybody like you, and always be happy." The instructions say to eat a complete breakfast with all the special people in your life, but Emmett doesn't have any special people in his life. He's behaving, but he has no relationships and no love.

No one notices Emmett. He's doing such a good job of fitting in that no one really knows him. When people are asked, they can't think of a single distinctive thing about him.

But then Emmett finds himself pulled into a countercultural movement of renegades who believe President Business is wrong. They're seeking to destroy the culture he has created. Instead of conformity, this group emphasizes the uniqueness of everyone and the distinct contribution only each individual can make. Emmett is told, instead of following the instructions, to "build something only you can build."

In this group Emmett discovers what he's been missing: relationships.

He also finds, for the first time, that he's free to admit his weaknesses and fears. Since he no longer has to be the same as and impress everyone else, he can just be himself. He can be authentic.

Emmett joins and eventually becomes a leader in this freedom movement.

In Jesus' Day

As odd as this may sound, the culture in Jesus' day was very similar.*

The Pharisees played the part of President Business. They were the religious leaders but acted like the religious police. With them, everything wasn't awesome; everything was rigid.

They wanted everyone to follow the instructions and to behave. It was all about the externals.

The problem is that God, whom they claimed to represent, really wants a relationship with people. But these religious leaders weren't leading people into a relationship with God; they were pushing conformity under their oppressive authority.

The Pharisees acted like they were perfect. They hid their flaws, which led everyone else to feel like they could never admit weakness or confess sin.

But then Jesus came along. And he started a countercultural

---

* Except it was real people, not LEGO people. In fact, LEGO blocks weren't even invented back then, nor was Will Ferrell.

movement, teaching that the Pharisees were wrong and seeking to destroy the religious culture they had created.

In one confrontation, Jesus said, "The teachers of religious law and the Pharisees are the official interpreters of the law of Moses. So practice and obey whatever they tell you, but don't follow their example. For they don't practice what they teach. They crush people with unbearable religious demands and never lift a finger to ease the burden."*

The Pharisees had made religion a burden, and that's wrong. Jesus taught that he came not to burden people but to set them free.

He continued, "What sorrow awaits you teachers of religious law and you Pharisees. Hypocrites! For you shut the door of the Kingdom of Heaven in people's faces. You won't go in yourselves, and you don't let others enter either."** The Pharisees were supposed to be helping people connect with God and go to heaven, but they were actually keeping people from God and heaven.

Jesus wouldn't let up:

What sorrow awaits you teachers of religious law and you Pharisees. Hypocrites! For you are so careful to clean the outside of the cup and the dish, but inside you are filthy— full of greed and self-indulgence! You blind Pharisee! First wash the inside of the cup and the dish, and then the outside will become clean, too.

What sorrow awaits you teachers of religious law and you Pharisees. Hypocrites! For you are like whitewashed tombs—beautiful on the outside but filled on the inside with dead people's bones and all sorts of impurity. Outwardly you look like righteous people, but inwardly your hearts are filled with hypocrisy and lawlessness."***

---

* Matthew 23:2-4.
** Matthew 23:13.
*** Matthew 23:25-28.

Whereas the Pharisees were about externals, Jesus cares about what's inside a person, about the heart. Jesus focuses on love and relationships.

And Jesus teaches people to be themselves. God's signature color is diversity. He loves it that people are different. And that means people can be authentic and make a unique contribution in the world.

Same as It Ever Was

What's really sad is that there are churches today where things seem very similar to how they were back in LEGO world under President Business and in the Bible times under the Pharisees.

Some churches teach that it's all about following the instructions. This is often called "legalism." It's a focus on externals and the demand that everyone should conform. Legalists think Christians all need to act the same and pretend they're happy, even if things aren't awesome. No matter what happens, just smile and say, "God is good."

Someone died? Just smile and say, "God is good!"

You're struggling with doubts? Just smile and say, "God is good!"

Sin has crept into your life? Don't tell anyone. Just pretend everything is awesome.

Too often, religious people can live as if Christianity is external and rule based, but what God wants is internal and relationship based.

External, rule-based religion tends to create cookie-cutter Christians. That's not God's desire. He created us to be individuals. He loves diversity. The only person we're supposed to model ourselves after is Jesus, and again, that's an internal thing, not external.

External, rule-based religion also tends to create hypocrites. Legalism encourages hypocrisy because we can cover up what's really happening on the inside by performing the externally right behaviors that are sure to impress people. But what God wants is for us to be authentic in our relationships so we can get the help we need.

External, rule-based religion is also wrong because it attempts to change the world through behavior modification, by wielding power and enforcing rules. The way Jesus changes the world, however, is through love. Christians don't work to change people's behavior; we love people despite their behavior. And when people truly experience that kind of love, it will change them from the inside out. The church's message is not one of enforcing morality but of offering mercy. Our message is not, "Stop messing up!" No, it's that God is head over heels in love with mess-ups, and that his love changes lives.

And you are being called. Jesus wants to bring you together with a ragtag group of renegades in a countercultural movement to offer freedom and meaning and community to a world that's desperate for it. Will you sign up? Will you give your life to God's mission of love?

•   •   •

Now What?

> Read John 8:34-36.

> The Pharisees focused on obedience to rules, and it drove people away from God. Jesus focused on love, and it drew people to God and led them to *want* to follow the rules. If a church followed Jesus' example and really focused on God's love for us, how might it better attract people and better lead them to truly live for God? How could you help make your church more like that?

➤ Pray today that God's love will change you from the inside out so that you become a person of godly character, increasing integrity, and Christlike compassion. Ask him to give you an internal desire to be more like Jesus.

Day 5

MORE THAN MEETS THE EYE

Let your good deeds shine out for all to see, so that
everyone will praise your heavenly Father.

MATTHEW 5:16

THE TRANSFORMERS MOVIE SERIES begins with high-school junior Sam Witwicky about to purchase his first car. He goes down to a used-car lot and buys a beat-up, canary-yellow Camaro. The odd thing is that the car seems to have a mind of its own. It will change radio stations or even just drive away independently.

Sam's car isn't the only machine taking action. A helicopter attacks US soldiers in Qatar by turning itself into a vicious robot. A boom box hacks into top-secret government files.

What is going on?

It turns out that they are "Transformers,"* which are actually robots in disguise. There are good Transformers called the Autobots and evil Transformers called Decepticons.

Both groups are searching for the Allspark, a cube that is their life source and that grants total power to anyone who possesses it. It

---

* Please say, "More than meets the eye" in your best robot voice.

turns out the Allspark was stashed on Earth years before. Sam's great-grandfather found it on an Arctic expedition, and it's been handed down to Sam, who has no idea what it is. But now he's dragged into this battle, which is really a race to save the planet. Most of the Earth is caught up in the middle of this war, even if they don't understand it. Slowly Sam begins to understand what's going on, and it gives him a chance to be a hero, to be a part of saving the planet and humanity.

Decepticons

I believe the Earth is a battlefield between good and evil.

I'm not talking about people.

I mean it's a battlefield between good and evil forces we don't fully understand and can't see.

The battle is over a sort of Allspark, the life source. I believe there is an otherworldly source of life available. His name is Jesus. A relationship with Jesus is the spark that gives true life.

The good side is trying to help the people of Earth recover this "Allspark." The evil side is trying to steal it away. Jesus said, "The thief's purpose is to steal and kill and destroy. My purpose is to give them a rich and satisfying life."*

The way the evil side tries to steal the life source away is through deception. The apostle Paul wrote to some Christians, "I fear that somehow your pure and undivided devotion to Christ will be corrupted, just as Eve was deceived by the cunning ways of the serpent."** The danger is that people will be deceived, which can happen because the evil side is all about deception.

There are all kinds of deceptions that can keep people from the life source, like "Jesus was just a good guy" and "You don't need a Savior" and "Don't give your life to God; he'll take all the fun out of it."

And if people are deceived, they miss out on life.

---

* John 10:10.
** 2 Corinthians 11:3.

More Than Meets the Eye

The problem is that people *have* been deceived. They've bought into the lies. The role of the church is to help people to overcome the deceptions of the evil side so they can find the life source.

How?

Transformation.

We can tell people all day what the truth is, but most of the time most people aren't going to listen. They can argue with our truth, or just ignore it.

What will really get their attention is transformation. When they see a person change before their eyes, it's just undeniable. When we connect with Jesus, he gives us incredible power. That power allows us to change. We join in the battle and become part of saving the world.

Once Jesus healed a man who had been blind from birth.* Skeptical people started denying the miracle, arguing that the man who could see couldn't be the same guy who was blind. The religious leaders were called in and realized Jesus did do a miracle. They felt their authority was being threatened by Jesus' increasing popularity, so they decided to drum up an accusation against Jesus. They argued that doing a miracle isn't appropriate on the Sabbath. They claimed that since Jesus wasn't resting on the Sabbath, he was a sinner. The guy who had just been healed was asked to give his opinion and said, "Whether he is a sinner or not, I don't know. One thing I do know. I was blind but now I see!"**

How can you argue with that?

You can't.

When Jesus transforms a person's life, it's undeniable. People can try to come up with some other explanation for the change they're seeing, but they start to realize it's just true.

So we need to be changed. It's part of how we save the world.

---

* See John 9.
** John 9:25, NIV.

How?

I wonder if you have the feeling that you can't change. A lot of people do.

Our past seems to prove it. We tried to lose weight, but the diet and workout plan got pushed aside after a while. We sought to manage our anger, but the breathing techniques turned into hyperventilating. We tried to be a better husband or wife or employee or son or daughter, but it seems like no matter what we have tried, it hasn't quite worked.

Why couldn't you experience lasting, significant change in the past?

My guess is that you focused on yourself, on what you could do through your power to change yourself. And my guess is that you focused on externals, on changing your behaviors.

You did it backward. But moving forward can be different, because it's going to be the opposite of what you did in the past.

It's not going to be you transforming you; it's going to be God. God is capable of doing anything, including changing you.

God's plan for transforming you doesn't focus on externals; it's about internals. God's not going to change you from the outside in, but from the inside out. That's the only way real, lasting transformation happens.

God can change you, and he wants to. He wants to because, although he loves you just as you are, he loves you too much to leave you that way. He wants you to become your best you. And not just for you. He wants others to see you change and to be drawn to him by it.

Your part in this process is to let him change you. To open yourself up to his transforming work in your life. More than just being open to it, you need to seek it. To invite God to come into your life and do what he needs to do to help you become the *you* he means for you to be.

The church is a community of people where the one constant is change. Where love is the atmosphere we live in, but we love each other too much to allow each other to stay the same. So we graciously encourage each other to be open to God's work in our lives. And a watching world sees the transformation and is drawn in by it.

• • •

Now What?

> Read 1 Peter 4:1-6.

> What changes have occurred in your life and character since you started following Jesus? Have other people noticed the changes? How has this impacted them?

> Pray again today for growing a godly character. Where is your character most in need of transformation? Pray for discernment with that. And pray that God will give you the desire to spend so much quality time with him that his character will rub off on yours.

WEEK SIX
Obstacles

*Some think believing in Jesus gives you a
free pass from struggle. Nope. Jesus said,
"In this world you will have trouble."*

*There are all kinds of obstacles we must overcome
as we move forward in our spiritual lives.*

What are those obstacles?

And how do we overcome them?

Day 1

THE BENEFIT OF THE DOUBT

I am confident I will see the LORD's goodness while I am here
in the land of the living. Wait patiently for the LORD. Be brave
and courageous. Yes, wait patiently for the LORD.

PSALM 27:13-14

I WANT YOU TO IMAGINE SOMETHING.

You're supposed to be meeting someone for lunch. You arrive at the restaurant five minutes early. You're asked if you'd like to get a table. You agree, sit down, and start looking over the menu. Finally, you look at your watch and realize ten minutes have gone by. Your friend is five minutes late. Another ten minutes go by and your friend is now fifteen minutes late. After another five, you come to the conclusion your friend isn't going to show up.

Question: How do you feel about your friend?

Answer: It depends which friend it is.

Right?

You have some friends where you would think, *Unbelievable! No, actually, this is totally believable! He is so unreliable. He's an insensitive jerk! Why did I even assume he was going to show up?* You would have real doubts about that friend.

But you have other friends where you would think, *Wow, this is so unlike him. Maybe he's sick. But he would have called. I hope he didn't get in a car accident.* You would give that friend the benefit of the doubt.

You wouldn't decide how to respond to your friend's tardiness based on that one incident. Your reaction would be based on what you already believe about your friend.

Where Is God?

One of the obstacles every Christian struggles with is doubt. It may be doubts about whether God exists. But more often, I think, our doubts stem from not understanding God. "Why isn't he answering my prayer?" "Why did he allow that to happen to me?" "Why doesn't he seem to care?"

It may help you to know that you're not alone. *Every* believer has a little doubt mixed in with his or her faith. In fact—and this may surprise you—the Bible is full of people who believed in God and loved God but didn't always *understand* God. People who had faith, but also had their faith challenged and had times of doubt and questioning God.

One of those people was Job.* Job was a man who loved God and had great integrity. He believed in and worshipped God, and then the bottom dropped out. Job lost everything but his wife. And it turns out his wife was no treat. In fact, Job's wife's encouragement was, "Job, just curse God and die."** Thanks, honey!

Job didn't curse God. He *did* struggle with God. He wrestled with God. He questioned God and even screamed up at the heavens.

We're not alone. Even giants of the faith sometimes experience giant questions and doubts.

---

* The name *Job* rhymes with *globe*. It's not *Job* that rhymes with *Rob*. Although the reality is, no matter how it's pronounced, it's just a weird name. Not as weird as Globe would be, but much weirder than Rob.
** See Job 2:9.

Job was confused and angry, but through it all, *he trusted God.* In fact, he said, "Though he slay me, yet will I hope in him."*

As someone who sometimes struggles with doubts, I want to know, how did Job continue to trust God when he didn't understand God at all?

I think Job was able to believe *in* God because he had already decided what he believed *about* God.

I'm not saying he understood God, because he didn't. And I'm not saying he didn't question God, because he did.

But in the days of crisis, Job wasn't developing his picture of God. He had already formed that picture, and he was confident about it. His confidence probably didn't make what he went through less painful, but because Job had already decided what he believed about God, he was able to give God the benefit of the doubt.

The same holds true for us. The best time for me to decide what I believe about God is not when I'm in the middle of some painful situation. The best time is now, because I've got a clear head now. So I need to develop an accurate picture of God now, and that accurate picture will help get me through my spiritual crises.

An Accurate Picture

The obvious question is: *How* do I develop an accurate picture of God?

It's difficult, because there are all kinds of people pointing us to all kinds of pictures of God. You'll hear that "God is mean and vindictive," and "God is tolerant and accepts everyone," and "God is running our lives like a puppeteer pulling the strings on a marionette," and "God is an absentee landlord who doesn't care what's going on in our lives."

So who do you listen to?

No one. You don't listen to anyone. Instead, you look at Jesus.

---

* Job 13:15, NIV.

One time Jesus was talking to people who wanted to know what God (the Father in heaven) is really like. He said,

> "If you had really known me, you would know who my Father is. From now on, you do know him and have seen him!"

Philip said, "Lord, show us the Father, and we will be satisfied."

Jesus replied, "Have I been with you all this time, Philip, and yet you still don't know who I am? Anyone who has seen me has seen the Father! So why are you asking me to show him to you? Don't you believe that I am in the Father and the Father is in me? The words I speak are not my own, but my Father who lives in me does his work through me."*

Jesus said, "I am your picture of God. If you see me, if you get to know me, you have seen God and know God." He was telling us that our understanding of God should be centered on him.

The Bible says this time and time again: "Christ is the visible image of the invisible God"** and "The Son radiates God's own glory and expresses the very character of God."***

The more we know Jesus, the more we know God himself. The more we experience Jesus, the more we experience God himself. In the books of Matthew, Mark, Luke, and John, the Bible gives us a very detailed picture of Jesus, which allows us to develop a very accurate picture of God.

And I'm convinced that being certain that God looks like Jesus is what can help us get through those times when we're confused.

Because when you look at the life of Jesus, you realize he was

---

* John 14:7-10.
** Colossians 1:15.
*** Hebrews 1:3.

amazing. His character, his love, his compassion, the way he cared for those who were hurting and cried when his friends cried, the way he treated people with grace and tenderness—amazing.

If God is like that, I can trust him no matter what's going on in my life.

And God is *exactly* like that.

That means when *you* have doubts, you can give him the benefit of the doubt.

• • •

Now What?

> Read Luke 7:18-28.

> This passage comes at a time when John the Baptist (who was the first to believe that Jesus is the Messiah) was in jail (for telling people about Jesus) and, apparently, he was struggling with some doubts. How did John handle his doubts about Jesus? How did Jesus handle John's doubts? What does all of it say to you about the times when you question God?

> It's been said that the most important thing about you is what you think of when you think of God. So praying for an accurate picture of God is *really* important. That should be something you regularly do. Why not start today?

Day 2

DOGS AT WAR

The temptations in your life are no different from what
others experience. And God is faithful. He will not allow the
temptation to be more than you can stand. When you are
tempted, he will show you a way out so that you can endure.

1 CORINTHIANS 10:13

WHEN I WAS A NEW CHRISTIAN, I read a story that totally impacted how I thought about living the Christian life. In fact, the principle I learned from it has been probably *the* essential factor in helping me to overcome one of the biggest obstacles every Jesus follower faces: temptation.

There was a small village in Alaska with no entertainment options. The most exciting thing happened every Saturday morning, when a man would bring his two dogs into town and have them fight until one dog couldn't fight anymore and the other was declared the winner.* All the locals would come out to watch and bet on a dog. Most would win about half their bets. But one man from the village began to notice that the owner of the dogs also bet every week, and got *every* bet right. He knew the dog owner was

---

* No, the man's name was not Michael Vick.

somehow fixing the fights, so he confronted him: "Listen, I know you're up to something. If you don't let me know what it is, I'm telling everyone this is fixed."

The owner of the dogs took a deep breath and said, "All right, I'll tell you, but don't tell anyone else. When I bring the dogs home from the fight on Saturday I feed both of them for four days, but from that point I stop feeding one. When I bring them into town on Saturday you can't tell the difference, but one of them is weak and one is strong because I've fed one and starved the other. And the one I feed always wins."

God's Power, Not Willpower

Most people try to battle temptation with willpower. I have a secret to tell you: temptation has more power than your willpower. If you try to battle temptation with willpower, you will be overpowered. If we put the problem and the solution into math equations, they might look like this:

$$\text{The Power of Temptation} > \text{Willpower}$$

$$\text{BUT}$$

$$\text{God's Power} > \text{The Power of Temptation}$$

You can't overcome temptation.* God can. And if you've given your life to God, he's given his life to you. He has given you his nature through his Holy Spirit inside you.

At the same time, you're still human and have your old nature that craves sin. And so . . . let's get ready to rumble! Here's how the Bible describes it:

---

* You can, however, overcome The Temptations. Not in a sing-off, but in a fight, because those dudes have gotten really old.

I say, let the Holy Spirit guide your lives. Then you won't be doing what your sinful nature craves. The sinful nature wants to do evil, which is just the opposite of what the Spirit wants. And the Spirit gives us desires that are the opposite of what the sinful nature desires. These two forces are constantly fighting each other, so you are not free to carry out your good intentions.*

So, when you're tempted, who will win? Will it be God's side, whispering in one ear, "Don't do it. Say no"? Or will it be the bad side, whispering in the other ear, "It's not a big deal. Everyone's doing it. Just do it once"? Who will win?

The side you feed always wins. And the side you starve always loses.

Think of a boxer. Whether or not he defeats his opponent doesn't depend on how much he wants to win when he gets in the ring or how hard he tries once the bell rings. Victory depends on his preparation before he ever gets in the ring.

When you're tempted, it's not about how much you want to be faithful or how hard you try to say no. It's all about what happened in the hours and days and weeks leading up to that moment. If you've been feeding the good side you will "let the Holy Spirit guide" your life when the moment of truth arrives.

So how do you feed the good side?

Every time you read the Bible, you feed the good side.

Every time you pray, you feed the good side.

Every time you memorize a Bible verse, you feed the good side.

Every time you serve God or other people, you feed the good side.

Every time you give money to God, you feed the good side.

Every time you spend time with and get encouragement from other Christians, you feed the good side.

---

* Galatians 5:16-17.

You may not realize it, but when you do those types of things, you're in training, gaining spiritual strength. When you're tempted, you'll be amazed that you have a power beyond your own that enables you to say no.

And it will be even better if you've been starving the bad side. How do you do that? It depends on what temptations you're susceptible to.

If you find yourself tempted sexually, there are some things you shouldn't be looking at.

If you're tempted to be greedy, you shouldn't drive through nice neighborhoods and stare at the houses.

If gossip is a weakness, maybe you need to think twice before talking to certain people.

If you have a short fuse, what is it that lights it? Perhaps you need to stop listening to the radio personality who gets you riled up, or stop checking your stocks, or quit playing in pickup basketball games.

If you're tempted to overeat, maybe cut out those weekly trips to the chocolate factory.

There is a war going on inside you. "Two forces are constantly fighting each other," and the battle is too important to lose.

The side you feed will always win.

•　　•　　•

Now What?

> Read Luke 4:1-13.

> What seemed to help Jesus overcome temptation? How could those same things help you in your battle against temptation?

➤ What temptations do you know you'll face today? This weekend? Ask God to give you his strength to overcome temptation.

Day 3

JUGGLING

Just as you sent me into the world, I am sending them into the world.

JOHN 17:18

LIVING IN LAS VEGAS, I've gotten to know one of the best jugglers in the world.

This guy can juggle three machetes while riding a unicycle.

I can juggle three tennis balls while standing on the ground.

When my kids were younger they would take two balls, start tossing them up and down, and shout, "Look, Daddy! I'm juggling!" I would explain to them that you have to juggle more than two things for it to be considered juggling.

Lately, though, I've reconsidered my position on juggling. I now think there *are* two things that if you can keep them both "in the air" at the same time qualify you as a juggler.

In the World, Not of the World

In John 17 we find Jesus praying. He is praying for us.

He prays for us because we are "in the world."* He tells his

---

* John 17:11, NIV.

Father that he does not want his followers taken "out of the world."*
In fact, he says he is sending us "into the world."** But he doesn't
want us to be "of the world."***

Reading it can be a little confusing.

When Jesus says that we are *not to be "of the world,"* he means
that we can't be like everyone else. People need to see a difference
in those who call themselves Christians. We should be set apart
by our character; our lives should be marked by love, joy, peace,
forbearance, kindness, goodness, faithfulness, gentleness, and self-
control.**** The Bible says that our lives should be so distinct that
people notice and are forced to ask questions.***** We are not to be
of the world, not to be the same as everyone else. We should live
question-provoking lives.

When Jesus says we are *to be "in the world,"* he means that we
can't isolate ourselves from everyone else. People who don't believe
need to be around people who do. We set ourselves apart by our
character, but we don't separate ourselves. In fact, the Bible says
that we are to be Christ's ambassadors to this world.****** Just as an
ambassador lives in another nation to represent his or her country,
we live in this world we are not a part of, and among its people, to
represent Jesus.

Reading Jesus' words in John 17 can be a little confusing.
Living them can be *really* confusing. Many Christians find it to be
a difficult obstacle to overcome—they either want to retreat from
the world, or they live in the world and are just like the world.
In fact, living in the world but not being of the world is kind of
like, well, juggling.

---

* John 17:15.
** John 17:18.
*** John 17:16, NIV.
**** See Galatians 5:22-23. When you read those verses, you'll notice that these qualities are called the "fruit
of the Spirit." The idea is that we don't work hard to manufacture these traits. Instead, they will be the
natural result of having the Holy Spirit inside us and staying connected to him.
***** See 1 Peter 3:15.
****** See 2 Corinthians 5:20.

A Flight to the Holy Land

A few years back I was able to go to the Holy Land.

It was a once-in-a-lifetime opportunity, so I decided to journal all of it. I would write down my impressions and what I learned about the land where Jesus lived.

I planned on writing once we arrived in Israel, but something happened when we got on the airplane that made me grab my journal. A Hasidic Jew was sitting across from me and making a spectacle of himself. Here's what I wrote:

He sits across the aisle from me all gray hair and gray curls and gray beard and black pants and black jacket and black hat. He is chanting. The moment he took his seat he began reading his Hebrew Scriptures. I grab the in-flight magazine to see what the movie might be.

Is he reading out loud, or praying, or singing?

What radio stations can I listen to with these headphones?

I get out my journal to do some calling on God of my own. The man is calling a flight attendant.

God, can you help me? I write.

"How can I help you?" the stewardess asks.

What can I learn from sitting next to this man? I ask God.

"I cannot sit by a woman," the man tells the flight attendant.

Let's see what she does about this, I think.

"Let me see what I can do about this," she says.

She walks away. He goes back to reading. I go back to writing. A young lady walks up and prepares to take the seat in front of me. I look up. He looks up. I look down. He looks up again. I look at him. He looks up again, and again, and again. He's checking her out! At least I think so. I'm pretty sure. No wonder he must sit next to a man. So is it good that he knows his weakness? Or is it bad that he has separated himself out of real life?

God, I don't want to be of this world, but I do want to be in it. I want to be both approachable and beyond reproach. I want to love you and people. I want to breathe you in and also breathe you out. I want to feel your touch and I want to be your touch.

God, help me to be like this man across the aisle, and please make sure I am not like him. More than anything, I want to be like Jesus.

Like Jesus

When you realize God is for you, it becomes enticing to want to pull yourself *out of* the world so you can put your focus more on him.

When you realize God is also for everyone else, it becomes imperative to put yourself *into* the world so you can help others put their faith in him.

It's challenging.

But it's encouraging to know that Jesus prayed for help for us to do it.

And it's essential for us to look at Jesus so we know *how* to do it. Because he was in the world but not of it. He kept his focus on God, and he helped others find faith in him.

I may be the first person to say it this way, but Jesus was a great juggler.

• • •

Now What?

> Read John 17:6-19.

> What is one way you are too much "of the world"? How could that change? And what is one way you're not "in the world" enough? How could that change?

> Isn't it amazing to know that Jesus prayed for you? One thing he prayed is that you would be in the world (not retreat from it, but have relationships with and influence on people who don't know God), but not of the world (not thinking and acting the way the world does). If Jesus prayed that for you, you should probably join him and pray that for yourself. Why don't you do that now?

Day 4

THE PROFOUND IN THE PROFANE

Be still, and know that I am God! I will be honored by every

nation. I will be honored throughout the world.

PSALM 46:10

A COUNSELOR ONCE TOLD ME I have ADD.

Well, I think that's what she said. I wasn't really paying attention.

Attention deficit disorder is an inability to maintain focus. People who struggle with it may *want* to keep their thoughts centered on one thing but can find themselves unable to do so. It's been estimated that about 11 percent of kids in the United States suffer from ADD.

What I want to draw your attention to, however, is another issue. It's far more prevalent, but almost never talked about. It seems that almost all Christians suffer from Spiritual Attention Deficit Disorder, and if you ask me, that is just SADD.*

As our love for God grows, we want to think about him, talk to him, worship him. God promises to be with us every moment;

---

* Do you see what I did right there?

we don't want to ignore him. Yet many mornings I have told God I was going to do my day with him and then I have forgotten about him until it was time to go to sleep. I'm just being honest. I hate it, but it's true.

I really *want* to focus on him, but I seem to be focus challenged.

And it's not just me. It's also the world I live in. You know, because you live in my world. We rush from place to place, media grasps for our attention at every turn, a gaggle of voices come at us from every direction.

It's tempting to think that it would be better to just get away. To not be "in the world." To withdraw from all the agitating interruptions so we can increase our intimacy with God.

But that's not the way God would have it.

And when God came to our world, that's not the way he had it.

It's Only Appropriate

In yesterday's devotion, I mentioned that I went on a trip to the Holy Land. One day our group walked the Via Dolorosa ("the way of suffering"), which is the path Jesus walked from his trial to his crucifixion. Along the way, there are fourteen "stations of the cross"—fourteen spots where it's believed that something significant happened. Some of these are incidents that are recorded in the Bible (like a man named Simon being forced to carry the cross) and some are not in the Bible but have become "tradition" (like a woman named Veronica coming out of the crowd to comfort Jesus). Immediately after our walk, I wrote this:

> When we began this holy walk, I was prepared to travel this path in a sacred focus.
>
> But quickly my attention was assaulted by a myriad of distractions. My first reaction was that all of it was unbelievably inappropriate. However, I then realized that

this was the path, with all the distractions, that Jesus had to walk. And that this is the path, with all the distractions, that I walk. So my attitude changed . . .

When people tried to sell me something, I thought, *You know, it would be inappropriate for it not to be this way.*

When all the noise pulled my attention away from Jesus, *It would be inappropriate for it not to be this way.*

When my view of the divine was obstructed by signs of politics and power, *It would be inappropriate for it not to be this way.*

When the bra and underwear stands gave the allure of sex, *It would be inappropriate for it not to be this way.*

When I realized that yesterday I had shopped and purchased things in a store on this holy path, without realizing at the time that I was standing in a holy place, *It would be inappropriate for it not to be this way.*

When my mind would not stop wandering, *It would be inappropriate for it not to be this way.*

Why?

Because Jesus' life and the circumstances and sights and sounds of his life were not clean and sterile, purified from the stain of this world. He did not have holiness served to him on a silver platter.

Why would I expect my life and the circumstances and sights and sounds of my life to be any different?

Jesus, please help me to find the profound in the profane; to hear your still, small voice in the rumbling, big volume of this world; to see you everywhere I go, slipping in and out of the crowds, peeking through life's circumstances; to know that this place, and every place, is a place to take off my sandals—for it is all holy ground.

Attention Deficit

Today you won't be traveling the Via Dolorosa that Jesus walked, but you *will* be walking with Jesus.

Our goal is to glue our attention on him, to stay in constant contact with him, to enjoy and live in an uninterrupted awareness of his presence.

Yet there may not be a single moment in your day when your attention isn't pulled away from him.

The distractions will be deafening and his voice just a whisper.

It will be unbelievably easy to miss the presence and unconditional love of God, even though that's the most essential thing you will need today.

So join me in praying: *Lord, help me to detect the holy in the hullabaloo, the profound in the profane. Help me in the speed of my day to be still and know that you are God. Heal me of my SADD.*

•   •   •

Now What?

> Read Psalm 46.

> Take some time to sit quietly and try to become as aware as you can of God's presence with you. How did it feel to be quiet? How might it help you to keep your focus on God's presence for the rest of the day if you started every morning by doing that?

> God is going to be with you every moment of your next twenty-four hours. Ask him to help you to remember that and to keep your focus on him.

Day 5

SPIRITUAL AMNESIA

I will always remind you of these things, even though you know

them and are firmly established in the truth you now have.

2 PETER 1:12, NIV

A CHRISTIAN AUTHOR NAMED JERRY BRIDGES often asks a question when he speaks at conferences. He inquires of his Christian audience, "Who is the gospel for?"

How would you answer that question? Who is the gospel for?

The unanimous answer Bridges receives is, "The gospel is for *non*-Christians. For people who haven't accepted Jesus yet."

And, of course, they're right.

The greatest need of someone who has not yet accepted Jesus is to hear, understand, and respond to the gospel.

But is the gospel only for non-Christians? No. That's Jerry Bridges's point. He teaches people, "Preach the gospel to yourself every day." He claims it may be the most important thing a Christian can do each day. I think he may be right. You see, we get spiritual amnesia. We forget. We forget that we don't deserve to be

God's children. We forget that we're sinners. We forget God's amazing grace. We forget that he loves us despite us.

And we *mustn't* forget. Because when we forget we can:

- stop appreciating God;

- cease to be grateful for his grace;

- become complacent spiritually;

- look down on other people for not being as special as we are;

- lose our passion for sharing his love with others.

We *mustn't* forget. So we need to remind ourselves.

Reminded

This idea that we forget and need reminders is a theme in the Bible. Throughout the Old Testament, we see people using physical reminders—things like stones of remembrance and altars—to make sure they don't forget what God has done for them. The author of Psalm 77 writes, "I will remember the deeds of the LORD."*

Repeatedly in the New Testament we find this idea of people forgetting and needing to hear it again:

- "I want to remind you of the gospel I preached to you, which you received and on which you have taken your stand."**

- "It is no trouble for me to write the same things to you again, and it is a safeguard for you."***

---

* Verse 11, NIV.
** 1 Corinthians 15:1, NIV.
*** Philippians 3:1, NIV.

- "I will always remind you of these things, even though you know them and are firmly established in the truth you now have."*

- "Though you already know all this, I want to remind you."***

We forget. We get spiritual amnesia. We need to be reminded: I am a sinner. I am worse than I want to admit, but I am loved more than I dare to imagine.

Do You Know Who You Are?

I think my favorite example of someone who thought of an effective and clever way to be reminded is the apostle John. This is the John who wrote the Gospel of John. I want you to check out a few things he wrote:

Jesus was troubled in spirit and testified, "I tell you the truth, one of you is going to betray me." His disciples stared at one another, at a loss to know which of them he meant. One of them, *the disciple whom Jesus loved*, was reclining next to him. Simon Peter motioned to this disciple and said, "Ask him which one he means." Leaning back against Jesus, he asked him, "Lord, who is it?"***

When Jesus saw his mother there, and *the disciple whom he loved* standing nearby, he said to his mother, "Dear woman, here is your son," and to the disciple, "Here is your mother." From that time on, this disciple took her into his home.****

---

* 2 Peter 1:12, NIV.
** Jude 1:5, NIV.
*** John 13:21-25, NIV. Italics mine.
**** John 19:26-27, NIV. Italics mine.

She came running to Simon Peter and the other disciple, *the one Jesus loved*, and said, "They have taken the Lord out of the tomb, and we don't know where they have put him!"*

The disciple whom Jesus loved said to Peter, "It is the Lord!"**

Peter turned and saw that *the disciple whom Jesus loved* was following them. (This was the one who had leaned back against Jesus at the supper and had said, "Lord, who is going to betray you?") When Peter saw him, he asked, "Lord, what about him?"***

Do you know who John is referring to each time he wrote, "the disciple whom Jesus loved?" Himself.

If you asked John, "Who are you?" He wouldn't say, "I am a disciple," or, "I am an author of one of the four Gospels," or, "The brother of James, son of Zebedee,"**** or, "I am John," or even, "I am a follower of Jesus." His answer would have been, "I am the one Jesus loves."

Why do you think he started calling himself that? Was it because Jesus loved him so much more than he loved everyone else? I bet not. Was he bragging? I doubt it. I think it was just a reminder of who he really was. It had become his primary identity in life. And he didn't want to forget. Calling himself "the one Jesus loved" was a constant reminder. He was fighting off spiritual amnesia. He was preaching the gospel to himself.

I like John's idea so much, I borrowed it from him for my kids' lives. I decided I wanted my kids' primary identity in life to be, "I am

---

* John 20:2, NIV. Italics mine.
** John 21:7, NIV. Italics mine.
*** John 21:20-21, NIV. Italics mine.
**** Yes, his father's name was Zebedee. How cool is that?

the one Jesus loves." I thought it might be the best gift I could give them. So the first words I spoke to each of them after their births, and the last thing I often say to them now before they go to sleep, is, "Do you know who you are? You are the one Jesus loves."

I want to give *you* a gift. It's the best gift I can give you.

So, do you know who you are?

Well, you are a sinner who has spent your life rebelling against and retreating from God. You chose to be an enemy of God. But because of his grace, he sent his Son to take the punishment you deserve. And his Son was glad to do it because . . .

You are the one Jesus loves.

•   •   •

Now What?

> Read 1 Timothy 1:15-17.

> Does it seem to you that Paul is preaching the gospel to himself? What might it look like for you to preach the gospel to yourself? How might it be beneficial?

> Spend some prayer time thanking God for loving you despite who you've been, where you've gone, and what you've done. Thank him that your sin doesn't define you and that his love for you does.

Questions

There are certain questions that . . . keep
some people from ever coming to faith; lead
some to walk away from their faith; have some
Christians scared to talk about their faith.

Many assume they are questions without good answers.
But there are good answers. Let's look at them.

Day 1

CAN THE BIBLE BE TRUSTED?

Above all, you must realize that no prophecy in Scripture ever came from

the prophet's own understanding, or from human initiative. No, those

prophets were moved by the Holy Spirit, and they spoke from God.

2 PETER 1:20-21

I HAD NEVER BEFORE TOUCHED A BIBLE. I opened it with no thought that it might be true. It was foreign to me, something to be made fun of, and most of all, a fable. Maybe the Bible claimed to be the Word of God, but the members of Milli Vanilli claimed to be great singers. And people in Chicago claim every year that the Cubs are going to win the World Series. I knew how the story of Jesus would start: "Once upon a time there lived a man named Jesus." Like any other tall tale, it would conveniently leave out the when and the where so no one could check the facts.

I turned to Luke, chapter three, verses one and two. "It was now the fifteenth year of the reign of Tiberius, the Roman emperor. Pontius Pilate was governor over Judea; Herod Antipas was ruler over Galilee; his brother Philip was ruler over Iturea and Traconitis; Lysanias was ruler over Abilene. Annas and Caiaphas were the high priests. At this time . . ."

What?

As I continued to read, I realized the Bible is full of whens and wheres. Turns out, Christianity is based on purported historical events.

The Bible was *begging* me to investigate. And I was into that kind of thing. I had always been into that kind of thing. That's why I was about to go to law school. So . . . I decided to investigate.

I thought I might be the first person to ever do so. I could be the downfall of Christianity—or at least make fun of Christians for believing in something I could prove was false.

Evidence?

The first thing I wondered was whether anyone outside the Bible from back around the time of Jesus wrote about Jesus. I thought if Jesus was going around doing miracles and dying and resurrecting, then someone other than just the Bible writers would have written about him. I assumed Jesus was a myth made up by some guys with an agenda, so the only mention of him would be in the Bible.

Wrong.

Turns out there are at least thirty-nine authors of ancient documents outside the Bible telling about Jesus. These authors confirm about one hundred different facts regarding Jesus' life, teachings, crucifixion, and even resurrection. So even if I could get rid of the Bible, I couldn't get rid of Jesus.

But turns out I *couldn't* get rid of the Bible. I figured it was pure fiction or full of legends that grew over time as they were handed down through the ages, kind of like the telephone game I played growing up. It didn't take me long to realize my assumption was fatally flawed.

The issue is that the Bible writers wrote way too early, and there are way too many ancient manuscript copies, for legends to have grown over time. And not only were the Gospels written soon after the events happened, we also have a lot of copies of those manuscripts.

That means we can compare them to each other and make sure they all say the same thing and that there was no telephone game happening. When I looked at the evidence, I just couldn't doubt that what we have today is what was originally written way back then.

That was confirmed when I read quote after quote by people who had done the research and come to the same conclusion. Like John Warwick Montgomery, distinguished professor of law, vice president for academic affairs, and chairman of the history department at Wilfred Laurier University in Canada, who wrote, "To be skeptical of the resultant text of the New Testament books is to allow all of classical antiquity to slip into obscurity, for no documents of the ancient period are as well attested bibliographically as the New Testament." In other words, if you doubt that what we have is the original New Testament, you also have to throw out all of written history from the beginning of time to the time of Christ. Because the New Testament has far more evidence to prove it's accurate than any other document up to that time.

Now I was confused. It was becoming hard for me to argue with the fact that the Bible was true. And I realized the Bible reads like it is true. When you read Greek mythology or American tall tales, they sound like made-up stories, featuring heroes with exaggerated power and goodness. But as I read the Bible, I noticed that all the main characters are presented with embarrassing human frailties. If people were just making up stories, wouldn't they make the heroes sound better?

I knew the Bible was supposed to be full of contradictions, so I investigated those. It turns out the Bible *doesn't* have contradictions. It has *differences*, different people giving different reports about the same events. Those differences sound, well, different. But they *aren't* contradictions.

The confirmations of Scripture's truthfulness aren't just inside the Bible. If you look *outside* the Bible, you find that there have been over 25,000 archaeological discoveries that validate Scripture.

Archaeological expert Nelson Glueck writes, "It may be stated categorically that no archaeological discovery has ever controverted a Biblical reference."

And the most convincing evidence of all was for the resurrection of Jesus. It has to be the most scrutinized event in history. More people have tried to disprove it than anything else, but it turns out Jesus really did rise from the dead. You can prove it.*

Inspired

The Bible says about itself, "All Scripture is inspired by God."**

At one point I would have laughed at the idea that the Bible contained the very words of God. Today, there's probably nothing I'm more convinced of. And not just because of the evidence, but because I've been reading and trying to live according to the Bible now for about a quarter of a century, and it has turned my life upside down.

It's natural to have doubts, but you can trust the Bible.

It's natural to feel intimidated, but you can have confidence when you talk about the Bible.

And you can be transformed by reading the Bible, because it is supernatural. It contains the very words of God.

• • •

Now What?

> Read 2 Timothy 3:14-17.

> If reading the Bible consistently is one of the keys for you to be transformed into the person you're supposed to be, you should have a plan for reading the Bible. So what's your

---

* For evidence of the resurrection of Jesus, you can read one (or more) of these books: N. T. Wright, *The Resurrection of the Son of God* (2003); Lee Strobel, *The Case for the Resurrection* (2010); Frank Morison, *Who Moved the Stone?* (1987); and Timothy Keller, *The Reason for God* (2008).
** 2 Timothy 3:16.

plan? Do you have a regular time and place where you read the Bible? Do you have a plan for what you're going to read? If not, why not commit to creating a plan?

> Your posture toward the Bible and knowledge of the Bible are keys to your spiritual growth. Ask God to give you a love for his Word and a desire to know it more and more.

Day 2

WHY WOULD GOD PROVIDE ONLY ONE WAY TO HIM?

I am the way, the truth, and the life. No one can

come to the Father except through me.

JOHN 14:6

YOU'VE SEEN THE BUMPER STICKERS featuring symbols from different religions and the message "Coexist."

You've probably heard people say things like, "All religions are equally valid" and "They're all teaching basically the same thing" and "They're all just different paths to the same God."

And you appreciate that sentiment. Well, I do, because these people just want everyone to get along. And everyone getting along is a good thing.

But what these people are saying is just not true. It can't be. All religions are equally protected, and should be. But that doesn't mean they're all equally valid. In fact, that claim doesn't even make sense. It's impossible. Those who say it mean well, but honestly, they just haven't done any studying. If they had, they'd discover that while there are some similarities among the world's religions, at their core they are dramatically different. If we're all worshiping the same God who has just revealed himself in different ways to different people, then we're all worshiping a god who either doesn't know who he is or isn't telling the truth.

Contradictions

You should study the world religions. You'll find that they contradict each other in very significant ways. For instance:

You have Christianity, which teaches there's only one God and he is a personal God. Then you have Buddhism, which teaches there's no such thing as a personal God. And you have Hinduism, which teaches that there are millions of gods.

Christianity teaches that eating meat is fine, but Hinduism teaches that eating meat is immoral.

Christianity teaches that Jesus is God. Islam teaches that Jesus was a great prophet but not God.

Christianity says we live and die only once before we enter eternal life, but Hindus and Buddhists and Taoists say we are reincarnated or reborn and will live many lives.

Basically every religion but one teaches, at its core, that people need to work their way *up* to God, seeking to earn his favor.* The core of Christianity is that people on their own are desperately lost, but that we have a God who desperately loves us. So God came *down* to us and died for us so he could offer us his *un*earned favor. The very core teaching of Christianity is in complete contradiction to the core teachings of the other world religions.

So . . . which is it?

The same God could not be telling people such contradictory things. They are not different paths God has given to us. They can't be.

All religions are *not* essentially the same and cannot be equally valid. Only one can be right, and the others have to be wrong, even if we don't like that.

---

* Through praying certain prayers, doing good deeds, giving alms, following a strict religious diet, or going through a series of reincarnations.

Which One?

So there can only be one religion that's right. And they all claim to be the one correct one.

Christianity claims to be the exclusive way to God too. In fact, Jesus once said, "I am the way, the truth, and the life. No one can come to the Father except through me."*

So the problem is that we've got all these religions claiming to be the right one, and what we choose is the most important decision of our lives. We're not talking about which box we check on the "religious preference" section of a form. We're talking about what we believe about life, about the point of our existence, and what happens to us after we die. We need to get this right! So what do we do?

We find out which religion is right. Which one is true?

This is where things get interesting. Because you'll discover that the other religions are based on the teachings of a person, not on historical events. And you can't really prove or disprove a person's teachings. If you want to gamble your life on that person being right, you can, but that's a big gamble.

And that's the difference with Christianity. Well, that's one of what I would consider two huge differences. One is that Christianity is unique in that it's based on grace—God loves you unconditionally, and you don't have to earn his favor; he offers it to you as a gift. The second is that Christianity is based on historical events. Therefore, Christianity begs to be investigated.

Christianity is not just based on the teachings of Jesus; it's also based on the resurrection of Jesus. And a person rising from the dead is something you can find evidence for or against.

In fact, that's exactly how I became a Christian. I spent a couple of months trying to disprove the Bible. What I discovered (to my dismay at the time) is that there are volumes of evidence that prove

* John 14:6.

the events of the Bible actually happened as the Bible says they did and that Jesus truly rose from the dead and proved that he really is who he claimed to be, the only way to God.

I also discovered that hundreds of people have tried to disprove Jesus as the one who defeated death and provides the only way to God, but once confronted by all the evidence, were convinced and became Christians. We're talking about incredibly intelligent, highly esteemed people. We're talking about Harvard Law professors,[*] and Oxford history professors,[**] and award-winning investigative journalists,[***] and world-renowned archaeologists,[****] who all studied the evidence and came to the conclusion that Jesus really rose from the dead and is the only way to God.

The claim that Jesus truly is the one way to God is not based on arrogance but on objective evidence.

So What?

If you're not yet a believer, you need to get this one right. And the cool thing is that you don't have to guess. Because God based Christianity on historical events that can be proven, you don't need to have a blind faith. You can study and have an intellectually robust faith that Jesus is the way and the truth and the life, and you can't get to God except through him.

If you are a believer, hopefully knowing this strengthens your faith. It should.

It should also lead you to want everyone to know Jesus. There's no other way for them, and we have the honor of getting to tell them and help them to know God and get to heaven.

Wow.

---

[*] Like Simon Greenleaf, who wrote a book called *The Testimony of the Evangelists*, sharing evidence establishing Jesus really is who he claimed to be.
[**] Like Thomas Arnold, author of the three-volume book *The History of Rome*.
[***] Like Lee Strobel, who has written books on the evidence like *The Case for Christ* and *The Case for Easter*.
[****] Like William Ramsay, who, after trying to discredit the Bible, ended up becoming a convinced believer and wrote at least fifteen books on the historicity of the Bible, including *Was Christ Born at Bethlehem?*

• • •

Now What?

> Read 1 Corinthians 15:1-20.

> How does the author (Paul) make the resurrection of Jesus the cornerstone of faith? What in this passage helps you to become even more convinced that Jesus truly rose from the dead?

> God's desire is that everyone would come home to a relationship with him through faith in Jesus. There are many parts of the world where other religions dominate and some where people have never even yet heard of Jesus. Pray that God will send out missionaries and Bibles to every corner of the world so everyone will have a chance to hear and respond to the gospel.

Day 3

WHY DOES GOD MAKE US FOLLOW SO MANY RULES?

It is for freedom that Christ has set us free.

GALATIANS 5:1, NIV

"Do you really want to have to follow all those rules?"

I've always hated rules. If there was a rule, I wanted to break it. I wanted to be free.

I hate rules in general, and there are some rules that seem pointless. In fact, some rules *are* pointless. There are some laws that are so dumb it's hard to believe they're real. In Oklahoma it's illegal to have a sleeping donkey in your bathtub after 7:00 p.m. Apparently in Alabama it's illegal to wear a fake mustache in church or to have an ice-cream cone in your back pocket. In California it's illegal to have a dog pursue a bear. There's a US federal law making it illegal to issue a fake Weather Service forecast.* In Zion, Illinois, it's illegal to give a cat or dog a lighted cigar. And in Baltimore, Maryland, it's illegal to take a lion to the movies.**

---

* By the way, the Weather Service is predicting a tsunami for your area next weekend!
** Now what am I supposed to do when I'm in Baltimore?

Some rules are dumb. But I've always been someone who wanted to break *any* rule because I wanted to be free.

I think a lot of people are that way, which is why people wonder why God had to fill the Bible with so many rules for us to follow.

And it is true that when you become a Christian, you're deciding that you will obey whatever God says.

We should obey God because he is God and he is worth obeying. But there's another reason for obeying God, and it may surprise you. We should obey God because he is all about freedom, and obeying him actually *increases* our freedom.

Captive

When God had the world the way he wanted, there was only *one* rule. God is not into rules.

You might wonder, *Well, why even one rule?*

I think the one rule was God's way of giving people the choice of making him the authority in their lives. The tangible way God did that was by telling people they couldn't eat the fruit of one particular tree. But at the heart of that rule was the heart of the people the rule was given to. Would they submit to God's authority, or would they choose to be their own authority?

You might wonder, *Why is it such a big deal to God that people submit to his authority?*

I'm convinced part of the reason is that God is all about freedom and knew we couldn't be free apart from him.

We tend to think of freedom as being independent from any restrictions, but the truth is that we *need* restrictions to truly be free.

Think of a fish. It's only free if it's restricted to water. If, in an attempt to experience freedom, it escapes the confinement of water, it will actually *lose* freedom and die.

Or think of a dog. If you want your dog to run free, you put a fence around your yard. Why? Because if it tries to run free without that confinement, it will likely get hit by a car, thus losing its freedom and dying.

Or think of a child. If a kid wants to be his own boss and therefore rebels against the loving confinements of his parents, he won't experience true freedom. His life will be a disaster.

We need certain restrictions to be truly free. And living life in God's love and under his authority liberates us to experience real freedom.

So God gave only one rule, but the first people, wanting to be free, rebelled against God's authority. They quickly discovered that it hadn't liberated them; they had actually become confined to a less-than-free life. Their descendants, the Israelites, continued to rebel against God, and they ended up enslaved in Egypt. Finally, desperate, they cried out to God. They were wrong. They wanted him back. They wanted to be free. God heard their cry and led them out of slavery.

And then . . . God gave them rules. It was at this point that God gave his laws, including the Ten Commandments.

What Do God's Rules Do?

It's important to note *when* God gave people rules. Why? Because the rules aren't designed to lead people into a relationship with God; they're designed to help people who already have a relationship with God to experience freedom within that relationship.

This is one of the biggest theological mistakes people make. Surveys have been done asking people, "When you die, will you go to heaven?" Most people say, "Yeah, I think so." When asked, "Why?" they often reply, "I do pretty well at keeping the Ten Commandments."

Well, the truth is you probably haven't done that well at keeping the Ten Commandments. But even if you have, so what? It has nothing to do with getting to heaven. Heaven is for people who have chosen to love and worship and have a relationship with God.

God didn't give the Ten Commandments to show the Israelites how to get into a relationship with him. He gave the Israelites the Ten Commandments because they had already decided to get into a relationship with him. They were rules to follow within their relationship, not to establish a relationship.

Think of it this way. Imagine you show up at my church in Vegas and ask some guy, "Are you married to Jennifer? The one who volunteers in the preschool class?" And the guy says, "Yeah, I think so." So you ask, "Why do you think so?" And the guy says, "Well, I've always been nice to her. I've never lied to her. Never hit her. One time I saw her at Starbucks and I bought her a coffee. I've never offended her. So, yeah, I'm pretty sure we're married."

What?

No, *I'm* married to Jennifer.

Keeping the rules with Jen doesn't make you married to Jen.

Being nice to Jen doesn't make you married to Jen.

I'm married to her. Not because I keep the rules of marriage, but because twenty years ago I asked her, and she said yes, and we went through a wedding ceremony. And I should keep the "rules" of marriage because I love her. But even if I don't keep the rules, we're still married.

And, in the same way, keeping the Ten Commandments, keeping God's rules, doesn't make me a Christian, and it won't get me into heaven. I'm a Christian, and I'll go to heaven because God asked me to be in a relationship with him, and twenty-five years ago I said yes, and then I went through the ceremony of baptism. And, yes, I should keep his rules because I love him. But even if I don't keep the rules, we still have the relationship and I'm still going to heaven. Because it has nothing to do with keeping the rules; it has to do with God in love giving his Son, and me believing in and accepting him.

God gives rules to his people because they're his people. That's why he puts a "fence" around their behavior.

It's like the way I set rules for my kids because they're my kids. I don't set rules for other people's kids. (I would like to set some rules for other people's kids. But I don't, because they're not my kids.) And my kids didn't become my kids by following my rules. They're already my kids, and I give them rules because they're in my family, not to let them know how to become a part of my family.

Free
God doesn't give rules to people to show them how to become his people. He gives rules because they are his people.

And God doesn't give us rules to restrict our freedom; he gives us rules (like any good parent) to help us experience true freedom. He gives us rules because he knows if we follow them we will be free from regrets, free from shame, free from addiction, free of secrets, free from pain and heartbreak.

God has always been about freedom. That's why it's a theme throughout the Bible. For instance, the Bible says, "The Lord is the Spirit, and wherever the Spirit of the Lord is, there is freedom"* and "It is for freedom that Christ has set us free"** and "You, my brothers and sisters, were called to be free."***

So I think the real question isn't "Do you really want to have to follow all those rules?" It's "Do you really want to be free?"

•   •   •

Now What?

> Read James 1:19-25.

> This passage refers to God's rules as a perfect law that sets us free. How have you found yourself losing freedom because

---

* 2 Corinthians 3:17.
** Galatians 5:1, NIV.
*** Galatians 5:13, NIV.

of not following God's rules? How do you think following God's rules could increase your freedom?

> God wants you to live under his authority, according to his truth, so you can truly be free. Pray for the wisdom and strength to truly live life God's way. Pray that others who don't believe will see your freedom and joy and want it, and so be drawn to God.

Day 4

WHAT ABOUT HEAVEN AND HELL?

Just as each person is destined to die once and after that comes judgment,

so also Christ was offered once for all time as a sacrifice to take away

the sins of many people. He will come again, not to deal with our sins,

but to bring salvation to all who are eagerly waiting for him.

HEBREWS 9:27-28

WHAT IF I TOLD YOU I've never been to Hawaii, but I believe the beaches are covered with gumdrops and the ocean is made of milk chocolate?

Or what if I told you I've never been to Alaska, but I'm sure it doesn't actually exist? There's just no way there could be a place that cold.

You'd think I was crazy. You can't make up what something real is like, and you can't claim something that's real doesn't exist. Well, heaven and hell are real.

Heaven

People tend to think of heaven as a place filled with . . . whatever they want it to be filled with. It's a never-ending party or vacation, depending on whether you prefer a party or a vacation.

Do you know where we get those ideas about heaven? We make

them up. And that's crazy, because heaven is real. And we don't have to make up what it's like, because the Bible tells us the truth about heaven.

Death is not an end for us; it's a doorway to a new kind of life. We are going to live forever, and heaven is life with God—after we die. You see, God is all about living with us, and he keeps moving closer and closer to us.

In Old Testament times, God established the Tabernacle, and later the Temple, as the places where people could be with him in a special way. But when Jesus was born, God moved right "into the neighborhood" in the person of Jesus. After Jesus' return to heaven, God moved inside us in the person of the Holy Spirit. When we die, he brings us to heaven to be even closer to him. And at the end of history, God is actually going to bring heaven and earth together. The apostle John describes that in his vision of what is to come:

> Then I saw a new heaven and a new earth, for the old heaven and the old earth had disappeared. And the sea was also gone. And I saw the holy city, the new Jerusalem, coming down from God out of heaven like a bride beautifully dressed for her husband.
>
> I heard a loud shout from the throne, saying, "Look, God's home is now among his people! He will live with them, and they will be his people. God himself will be with them. He will wipe every tear from their eyes, and there will be no more death or sorrow or crying or pain. All these things are gone forever."*

So the main point isn't *where* heaven is; it's *what* it is. Heaven is living with God in eternal life. What is eternal life? Jesus said, when he was talking to God the Father, "This is eternal life: that

---

* Revelation 21:1-4.

they know you, the only true God, and Jesus Christ, whom you have sent."* Eternal life is life with God.

You can start experiencing it now. And you can experience it *fully* forever.

I heard a pastor named John Ortberg say, "Heaven does not contain God. God contains heaven." The apostle John describes it this way: "I did not see a temple in the city, because the Lord God Almighty and the Lamb are its temple. The city does not need the sun or the moon to shine on it, for the glory of God gives it light, and the Lamb is its lamp."**

In heaven, it will be impossible to avoid God. So if you don't want to be around God, you won't want to be in heaven. Heaven is the kind of place where people who want to sin would be miserable. Kind of like a person who is deeply addicted to nicotine having to go for a long dinner to a restaurant where there's no smoking. If you don't smoke, that restaurant would be great; it would be a breath of fresh air. But if you're addicted to smoking, you'd be miserable there.

People think that heaven is this eternal party, and that everyone wants in, but that God is going to keep some people out. But the reality is that heaven is where we live with God, and most people *don't* want it. But the amazing thing about God is that he's inviting *everyone* in. In fact, he sent Jesus to die to remove our sins so we can get in. And if we say yes to his invitation, he starts working in our lives, moving us toward becoming the kind of people who love him more than sin, who don't want to sin, and who someday will love being with him in heaven.

Hell

So, what is hell? Hell is the place where God is not.

In this world, in this life, people get to experience some of God's presence and some of God's goodness, even if they don't want to.

---

* John 17:3, NIV.
** Revelation 21:22-23, NIV.

God made the world and gave us life, and it's all drenched in his goodness. That's what love is, and laughter, and sunsets, and the coo of a baby, and a bird soaring across the sky, and the vibrant colors you see in the produce section of the grocery store, and the pleasure you feel in accomplishing a job well done or having sexual intimacy with your spouse.

In this world, in this life, we experience some of God's presence and God's goodness. But hell is the place where God and his goodness are not.

In the same way that God's presence is what makes heaven, heaven, God's absence is what makes hell, hell.

I want to show you a verse about hell, and it will probably make you uncomfortable. It makes *me* uncomfortable. Here it is: "They will be punished with eternal destruction, forever separated from the Lord and from his glorious power."*

Why "punished"? Well, because people sin and deserve punishment. We all believe that. If you heard about a guy who committed horrible crimes, and the judge let him go without punishment, that wouldn't make you happy. You would be upset because you know there should be justice. We have an amazing ability to downplay our sins, but the Bible says they're worse than we admit, and sin deserves punishment.

God is a fair judge, and he can't let our sin go without punishment.

God is also love, so he came and died on a cross for us and allowed Jesus to suffer the punishment we deserve for our sins.**

That uncomfortable verse said "punished," but did you notice it also said hell is being "separated from the Lord"? That's what hell is. God's absence is what makes hell, hell.

---

* 2 Thessalonians 1:9.

** Romans 3:26 (NIV) says God is "just and the one who justifies those who have faith in Jesus." To be "justified" means to be declared not guilty. God is just. He must punish sin. But God wants to justify us—to declare us not guilty of our sin. The only way he could do that is to have someone else take the punishment we deserve. That's what Jesus did. If we accept his dying as our punishment, we are declared not guilty and escape the punishment we deserve.

People ask, "Would a loving God really send people to hell?" The answer? He doesn't. God doesn't send people to hell. People choose to go to hell.

People will be in hell because they chose to be. Because they didn't want life with God.

The Invitation

But Jesus came to invite people to heaven. He's inviting everyone.

And once we say yes to God, we become one of the ways God invites people. The Bible says we become God's "ambassadors." We're like citizens of heaven, living on earth, representing God and inviting them to join him in heaven. "We are Christ's ambassadors; God is making his appeal through us. We speak for Christ when we plead, 'Come back to God!'"*

God's offer is to use us for the most important mission in the world; and what an invitation that is!

•   •   •

Now What?

➤ Read Revelation 21:1-27.

➤ Every day we're becoming something—either the kind of person who loves God more and sin less, or the kind of person who loves sin more and God less. We want to become the kind of people who will fit into and love heaven. So what could you do this week to become the kind of person who wants more of God and life with him?

* 2 Corinthians 5:20.

➤ In heaven, the presence of God will be so great you won't want to sin and you will want to worship him. Ask God to increasingly transform you into that kind of person, starting now. Pray for an awareness of his presence, for a disdain for sin, and for an overwhelming urge to worship him.

Day 5

WHY DOES GOD ALLOW EVIL AND SUFFERING?

Here on earth you will have many trials and sorrows.

But take heart, because I have overcome the world.

JOHN 16:33

A FEW YEARS AGO my family ate at a BBQ restaurant. As I was finishing, my stomach began to let me know something was wrong. I excused myself and walked—well, I ran—to the bathroom. I came out . . . thirty minutes later. I gave a report. "It's not good. I'm not done. Let's drive home during this . . . intermission." We got in the car. Unfortunately it was about a twenty-minute drive to our house. It was not a good trip. At one point I started screaming, "Why, God? I'll do anything, God! I'm suffering here, God! Can't you help me? What's happening, God? Why, God?"

The restaurant has since closed.*

Not Funny

That story is humorous, but suffering rarely is. And I'm sure you have stories that aren't funny at all:

Of your parents' divorce.

---

* I wonder why.

Of a loved one dying of cancer.

Of being the victim of abuse.

Of your spouse leaving you.

And of course there's pain and suffering on a more global scale: children starving, wars, babies orphaned due to the AIDS epidemic in Africa.

It's impossible to avoid the question: If God is good, why is there so much suffering?

And more personally, and probably more pressing: Where is God when I hurt?

Cry

There's a story in the Bible where two sisters named Mary and Martha send a message to Jesus that their brother, Lazarus, is on his deathbed. They're hoping Jesus will show up and heal Lazarus. They have seen Jesus heal people before.

Jesus shows up almost a week later, but Lazarus has already been dead four days. The sisters, Mary and Martha, each meet Jesus with an accusation: "If you had been here, my brother would not have died."*

It's what we do too. When we suffer, it's easy to blame God.

In Week 1, I mentioned the time I got the call in the middle of the night from my friend Rich, whose daughter had just died in a car accident. I raced to their house. It was my first time in that kind of situation. I didn't know what to say. Today, years later, with a lot more experience, I still wouldn't know what to say. I understand that horrible things happen not because God causes them—he doesn't; they're not part of God's plan. They happen because God gave people free will. For there to be freely chosen love, we have to have free will. And freely chosen love is the whole point. But free will means that people can make wrong choices, that everything can

---

* See John 11:21 and 32.

get messed up, and it has. Unfortunately, understanding the reason evil and suffering happen in our world doesn't help when we're in the middle of it.

Mary and Martha indicted Jesus. He saw their pain. The next line says, "Jesus wept."*

In the movie *Selma* there's a moment when Martin Luther King Jr. comforts a father who just lost his son: "There are no words. But I can tell you one thing for certain . . . that God was the first to cry. He was the first to cry for your boy."

When we suffer, God is the first to cry.

All I could do was sit with Rich and Karen and cry with them. And God was crying with us.

Happy Ending

It's comforting to know God cries with us, but it doesn't feel like quite enough. And that's why the rest of this story is so powerful.

After crying, Jesus walks to the grave of Lazarus, he calls out to him, and Lazarus comes out of the grave. A moment ago he was dead, but now he is alive.**

Jesus cried, but he did more than that. He cared for Mary and Martha. He took action. He met their need by raising Lazarus from the dead.

This is such a great lesson for us, because part of the pain when we suffer is that it seems like God has his eyes shut. But this story helps us see that God's eyes are not shut. God knows what we are going through. And just as Jesus relieved the pain of Mary and Martha, a day is coming when God will relieve our pain. In fact, we're promised that God will wipe away every tear from our eyes.***

* John 11:35.
** See John 11:38-44.
*** See Revelation 21:4.

Waiting

When you're suffering, it's hard to imagine the possibility of a happy ending.

But that's a lesson from the life and death (and life again) of Lazarus. I think we need to learn from the waiting period in the story, the four days when Lazarus's body was in the grave and his family cried and Jesus seemed callous. The four days of defeat, when Jesus didn't show up and didn't seem to care.

Those four days parallel the times when we face our pain and feel forgotten. For us it might be days or perhaps years of seeming defeat.

Looking at Lazarus's story from this side of history, we can see how after four days of defeat, the story has a triumphant ending. In his timing, God took action. Lazarus returned to life; everyone rejoiced. Jesus *had* cared. He wasn't callous.

We may have to wait far longer than four days, but if we love God, we have the promise of a personal solution ending in triumph. "We know that God causes everything to work together for the good of those who love God and are called according to his purpose for them."* Every question you've asked and every prayer you've prayed has been heard, and you *will* have a happy ending.

Even Now

Someday God will shake our Etch A Sketches, and the problems we've gone through will dissolve into a new painless picture. But until then, we don't just wait. God can do some pretty cool things, even through our suffering, even now.

When Jesus showed up at Lazarus's funeral, many people were gathered and watched everything go down. The result? "Many of the people who were with Mary believed in Jesus when they saw

* Romans 8:28.

this happen."* Incredible! The friends and family of Mary, Martha, and Lazarus became believers in Jesus because of Lazarus's death, because of Jesus' delay in showing up, and because Jesus raised Lazarus from the dead.

I told you that when Rich and Karen lost Megan, it felt like the end of the world. What I didn't tell you is that despite their confusion, they stuck close to God and were surrounded by supportive friends. And eventually they experienced healing. And they grew. Their faith grew. Their compassion for hurting people grew. Their marriage grew. And God ended up using them to comfort several other parents who lost children, and later to start a church where the compassion that oozed out of them drew all kinds of people to Jesus.

I've seen it happen over and over. Eventually, God will bring about the ending we pray for. In the meantime, if we're open to it, if we're open to him, God will do some cool things in our lives, even now, even through our suffering.

•   •   •

Now What?

> Read Romans 8:28-39.

> How could you keep the perspective that God is for you and with you even when you're suffering? How could that perspective help you to have a different attitude in the midst of pain?

> We live in a painful world. Belonging to God doesn't shield us from pain, but it does mean we get to go through it with

---

* John 11:45.

him. There are a lot of people who don't know God and are struggling through difficulties alone. Ask God to show you a person or two he's put in your life whom you could come alongside in their struggle. Ask him to show you how you can be Jesus to those people.

Mission

What does Jesus want his followers
doing? What's our priority?

And how do we do it? Especially if we're
new to this or nervous about it?

And if we do engage in the mission, how will our lives
be changed, and how might we change the world?

Day 1

SPLAGNA

When he saw the crowds, he had compassion on them because they
were confused and helpless, like sheep without a shepherd.

MATTHEW 9:36

WHAT DRIVES YOU?

What is the overriding passion of your life?

When you're falling asleep, what do you often find yourself
thinking about?

And when you wake up, what topic is still there, like a song
stuck in your mind?

If you had lots of extra time or money, what would you invest
it in?

I'm asking: What drives you?

What Drove Jesus

What drove Jesus?

That's an easy question to answer, because Jesus didn't leave it up

for debate. He said he came to seek and to save God's lost children.*
It wasn't just his official "mission statement." It was his passion. It
was in his guts.

> Jesus traveled through all the towns and villages of that
> area, teaching in the synagogues and announcing the
> Good News about the Kingdom. And he healed every
> kind of disease and illness. When he saw the crowds, he
> had compassion on them because they were confused and
> helpless, like sheep without a shepherd. He said to his
> disciples, "The harvest is great, but the workers are few.
> So pray to the Lord who is in charge of the harvest; ask
> him to send more workers into his fields."**

Jesus saw people whom no one seemed to care about. No one
was giving them attention or trying to help them; they were "confused and helpless." They were "like sheep without a shepherd."
They were people without their heavenly Father. They didn't have
God in their lives.

We're told that Jesus had "compassion" on them. The word *compassion* is translated into our language from the Greek word *splagna*.
Splagna is translated "compassion," but the word *splagna* literally
refers to intestines. What Jesus felt for these people wasn't a surface
emotion; it was gut deep. Jesus saw people who didn't have God,
and it made him sick to his stomach.

He couldn't just sit and watch. So he turned to his disciples
and asked them to pray that there would be people with enough
compassion to do something about it. To pray that he would have
followers who experience *splagna* and are driven by his mission of
seeking and saving God's lost children.

---

* See Luke 19:10.
** Matthew 9:35-38.

Our Mission

Jesus' mission is our mission. He said, "As the Father has sent me, so I am sending you."*

We need to make sure everyone knows there is a Father who loves them and is offering life to them through a relationship with him. For someone who has a relationship with God through Jesus, the most important thing is helping other people find it.

In fact, the very last thing Jesus said before he went back to heaven was, "Go and make disciples of all nations, baptizing them in the name of the Father and of the Son and of the Holy Spirit, and teaching them to obey everything I have commanded you. And surely I am with you always, to the very end of the age."**

He said, "Make disciples." A disciple is someone who has devoted his or her life to learning from and following someone.

He said when someone decides to become his follower, that person gets baptized. In baptism, the way many churches do it, a person gets lowered under water and then raised out of water. The symbolism is that it's like you're being lowered into a grave and then coming out of the grave to live a new life.*** It's a new life that's bigger and better because it's got Jesus at the center. Baptism is almost like a wedding; it's a ceremony you go through signifying that you are giving your life to a relationship with God.

Jesus tells us to live out the adventure of sharing God's love and Good News with others, and he offers to do it with us. He promises to be "with us always" as we engage in the mission.

Excuses

Jesus commanded that every Christian seek and save the lost, but many Christians ignore that command. Research indicates that the majority of Christians will never talk to others about their faith.

* John 20:21.
** Matthew 28:19-20, NIV.
*** See Romans 6:1-5.

Some don't because they consider their faith to be a private thing. Which, honestly, is ridiculous. If you had a cure for cancer, would you consider that a private thing? Would you keep it to yourself? Of course you wouldn't. We have what everyone needs—the love of God, a relationship with God, life with God, eternity with God—and we need to share that with everyone.

Christians make all kinds of excuses as to why we can't talk to people about our faith and try to help them to know Jesus.

"I can't do that because my life isn't a good enough example."

"I can't share Jesus because I'm not very good at that."

"I can't talk about my faith because I wouldn't know what to say."

"I can't tell people about Jesus because I wouldn't know the answers to their questions."

But none of those excuses are legitimate, because they're all about us. *I* is the common word in all of them. And *I* don't lead people to Jesus. God does. I have a part to play. I get to share Jesus with people. But I can't lead a person to Jesus. Only God can do that. So I don't need to worry if I can do it right or if I know the right words. I just do my best, I do my part, and God is the one who will lead people to Jesus.

We make excuses, worrying that we'll look silly or someone might not be happy with us if we talk about our faith. But considering how important it is for everyone to know Jesus, our excuses just don't hold up.

Did you know that in some countries today people get killed for talking about Jesus, but they don't use that as an excuse? They still do it. We have our excuses, but in America, no one will kill us for talking about our faith.

I realize our excuses feel real, but they're not as real as the people who need Jesus. Maybe what we need to do is pray for more *splagna*. Because if we had enough compassion, we would overcome our excuses and share our faith.

What Drives You?

So what drives you?

If it's not Jesus' mission, pray for that.

And: What are you going to do about it?

I've decided to give my life to Jesus' mission. And I'll tell you this: giving my life to Jesus' mission is the best decision I've made since giving my life to Jesus.

If you've given your life to Jesus, give the rest of it to his mission of seeking and saving God's lost children. In the end, it will be the only thing that really matters.

● ● ●

Now What?

> Read Exodus 3:1-14 and 4:1-17.

> God asks Moses to represent him and speak for him, but Moses makes excuses for why he can't. How does God overcome Moses' excuses? What excuses do you make for not representing God and speaking about him to others? How do you think God might overcome your excuses?

> God's burning passion is that his lost children would come home to him. Ask God to have the same passion burn in you. Ask him to break your heart for the things that break his heart.

Day 2

IT'S GOD'S KINDNESS

Don't you see how wonderfully kind, tolerant, and patient God

is with you? Does this mean nothing to you? Can't you see that

his kindness is intended to turn you from your sin?

Romans 2:4

ONE TIME AFTER A CHURCH SERVICE a lady bounced up to me and said, "Hey!"

I said, "Hey!"

"My name's Sandy," she said very quickly, "but not for long it isn't. I'm changing it! It's been a bad year for Sandys—Hurricane Sandy, Sandy Hook Elementary."

I nodded, a bit confused.

"So, hey!" Sandy continued. "I just wanted to thank you for keeping it positive."

I asked what she meant.

Sandy (or whatever her new name would be) said, "I went to church a few times growing up, and I've gone a couple of times as an adult, and I hate it. Hate it! You always feel like you're being judged. People look down on you. It's all negative. It's all about their rules. Don't do this. Don't do that. They tell me I have to dress appropriately. I've always hated church, but I've always wanted to know Jesus. So when I heard about this church, I decided I would check it out one time, and it was great! Thanks for keeping it positive. I'll be back next week!"

God's Way

Christians want other people to live God's way.

There are really good reasons for that. Living God's way honors God, and God deserves that. Living God's way is the best way to live, and we need that. Living God's way can encourage others to stay on the right path rather than distract them from it, and they appreciate that.

So what many Christians do is expect other people to behave. And tell other people to behave. And sometimes judge the people who aren't behaving.

But that just doesn't make sense. And it doesn't work.

If people aren't Christians, it doesn't make sense to expect them to live by God's standards. And without having the Holy Spirit to empower them, they're *incapable* of living up to God's standards. Besides, the Bible instructs us not to judge people who are not followers of Jesus.*

People who are Christians *are* expected to live by God's standards, and because they have the Holy Spirit, they are capable of living by them. But too often the way we communicate those expectations is pretty negative. Is fear (of the judgment of others, or even of God himself) really the best motivator for obedience? Think of it this way: What if you asked me if I would ever consider cheating on my wife? And what if my response was, "No way. I mean, I would, but she'd kill me!" That's *not* the best answer. Wouldn't it be better if I said, "No way. I mean, I love her so much, I could never do something like that"?

---

* See, for instance, 1 Corinthians 5:12.

The best motivation for holiness is love.

It's also the most effective.

Sandy

Sandy (who I later discovered was a Britney Spears impersonator who sang and danced provocatively in a casino on the Strip) kept coming back to our church, week after week. She never changed her name and never missed a service.

Several months later, I did a message on having purity in your marriage. I spent half the sermon talking to our single people. I explained that they could have purity in their marriages later by having purity before marriage now. So I urged them not to sleep with anyone until they got married.

In the middle of the message, I noticed Sandy sitting in the second row. I thought, *She is never coming back after hearing me tell her she can't have sex until she's married. She's going to say we're another one of those negative churches. I wonder if she's the type to just storm out, or if she's the type to come up and let me have it, then storm out.*

After the service, Sandy immediately walked toward me. I thought, *She's the type to let me have it and then storm out.*

I greeted her, "Hey, Sandy?" (I wasn't sure if she was still going with Sandy.)

"Vince," she said, "I'm getting baptized!"

"Huh?" was all I could get out.

"Yes!" she nearly shouted. "Since coming here my life has completely changed. If I explained it to you, I would start crying." She started crying. "The way I think about *everything* has changed. The way I think about God, about myself, about life. So I am giving my life to God, and I am getting baptized!"

Sandy got baptized and soon began to change everything about her life—without anyone telling her to. She broke up with her boyfriend. She quit her job.

Later, someone asked how it all happened. She said, "I heard Vince say, 'God has so much love for you.' And I just remember thinking, 'I never knew that. And I felt it for the first time, and it just opened up a whole new life for me.'"

God's Kindness

What happened with Sandy? Why did she make all those changes without anyone demanding that she behave, without anyone judging her or making her feel guilty?

What happened is *exactly* what the Bible says will happen.

> The grace of God has appeared that offers salvation to all people. It teaches us to say "No" to ungodliness and worldly passions, and to live self-controlled, upright and godly lives in this present age.*

We're told the *grace* of God has appeared. Not the *truth* of God, not the *wrath* of God, but the *grace* of God. That grace offers us salvation. Every Christian would agree with that. Then the Bible says that grace teaches us "to say 'No' to ungodliness and worldly passions, and to live self-controlled, upright and godly lives."

So according to the Bible, what leads people to stop sinning and to live holy lives? God's *grace*. His unmerited love.

> So when you, a mere human being, pass judgment on them and yet do the same things, do you think you will escape God's judgment? Or do you show contempt for the riches of his kindness, forbearance and patience, not realizing that God's kindness is intended to lead you to repentance?**

---

* Titus 2:11-12, NIV.
** Romans 2:3-4, NIV.

We're taught that, as sinners, we can't judge others. And that it's God's *kindness* that leads people to repentance.

So if we want to lead people to Jesus, our best approach is to lead with love. I don't think anyone has ever been judged into a relationship with God. Go out and love people. God's kindness will lead them to repentance.

You

And, by the way, this applies to you as well.

Maybe you truly want to live a holy life for God, but you've got this obstacle called sin. Sin has been keeping you from living faithfully for God.

What do you do?

You can focus on feeling judged and guilty. Chances are it won't be effective. If somehow it were, you might get to a place where you think, *I have to stop sinning. I mean, I want to keep doing it, but God might kill me!* But that is not the best motivator for obedience.

Instead, what if you focus on God's grace? Chances are it will be much more effective and get you to a place where you realize, *I stopped sinning. I mean, I just love God so much, I couldn't keep doing it.*

Focus on God's love. His grace will lead you to say no to ungodliness, and his kindness will lead you to repentance.

•　　•　　•

Now What?

> Read Titus 2:11-12 and Romans 2:3-4.

> Many Bible translations use the word *repentance* in Romans 2:4. To repent means to turn around. Where

does your life need a turnaround? Where do you need to change? How can you picture God's grace and kindness leading you to make that change? And how can you show God's love to others?

> Ask God to show you two people he has put in your life who are living their lives without him. Ask him to show you specific ways you can show his kindness to these two people.

Day 3

NO DARKNESS

You are the light of the world—like a city on a
hilltop that cannot be hidden.

MATTHEW 5:14

MISSIONARIES FASCINATE ME. These Christians are so passionate about God that they'll move across the world to a place they've never been and where they can't speak the language, all to help people in that place get to know God and get close to him. And they do this at a huge personal cost. In fact, it can cost them their lives.

Back in the early twentieth century, there was a group of missionaries known as "one-way missionaries" because they packed all their earthly belongings into coffins and purchased one-way tickets when they departed for the mission field. They knew they would never return home. Best-case scenario was that they'd be accepted and be able to live with the people there and help people there get close to God. But sometimes it didn't go so well, and they would contract a deadly disease or even be killed upon arrival.

The story is told of one such missionary named Peter Milnewho who felt called to a tribe of cannibals in the New Hebrides. He lived among the tribe for fifty-five years, until his death. A sign under his picture in the church he founded reads, "When he came there was no light. When he left there was no darkness."

Salt and Light

I am a fan of missionaries. I'm a bigger fan of salt. You might say I have a salt problem. I might say salt is glorious and one of God's best gifts.* You might say, "If you love salt so much, why don't you marry it?" I might say that I checked, and it's not legal in any state I've lived in.

As a lover of sodium chloride, it makes me very happy that Jesus spoke about salt.**

> You are the salt of the earth. But if the salt loses its saltiness, how can it be made salty again? It is no longer good for anything, except to be thrown out and trampled underfoot.
>
> You are the light of the world. A town built on a hill cannot be hidden. Neither do people light a lamp and put it under a bowl. Instead they put it on its stand, and it gives light to everyone in the house. In the same way, let your light shine before others, that they may see your good deeds and glorify your Father in heaven.***

Salt needs to have contact with food to add flavor.
Light shines brightest in the darkness.
To play our part, we *must* have contact with people who are far from God. We must get out of our safe places so we can shine light in the darkness.

---

* To answer your question, no, I don't have high blood pressure. And to answer your other question, yes, my favorite food is a salt bagel.
** Though he did not speak of it with as much affection as I believe he could have. I'm not one to typically question Jesus, but no one messes with my salt.
*** Matthew 5:13-16, NIV.

Light in Darkness

My wife, Jen, is completing her master's degree in counseling. After twelve years of staying home to raise our kids, she went back to school to get equipped to help hurting people.

She recently started her first internship. She's working at a secular counseling agency. She was criticized by some fellow students from the Christian university she's attending. They called her decision dumb, a waste. Why wouldn't she work at a Christian counseling center? She could counsel Christians. In a secular counseling center she couldn't talk about God unless the client brought God up first and wanted him included in their counseling.

Guess what? She's been working there for half a year, and just about *every* client brings up God, and when she asks, they *do* want to include God in their counseling. They're almost all non-Christians, but they're hungry, they're hurting, and they're open to any help they can get. So Jen gets to tell them about God's love and how he can be their refuge.

You know what I call that?

Being light in the darkness.

We Make Choices

We make choices every day that determine whether we'll function in the salt-and-light role Jesus has for us, or if we'll refuse him. To be salt and light, we must live lives that are distinct from those without Christ, and we must live our lives *with* those who are without Christ. So . . .

Will you join in the gossip by the coffeepot at work, or will you graciously walk away?

When there's someone left out, will you stay with the popular crowd, or will you show Jesus' compassion to the one who's been forgotten?

Will you join in the lustful talk about the receptionist who wears short skirts, or will you take the high road and show some dignity?

And whom will you invite over for dinner? The person from church whom you have God in common with, or the person who doesn't go to church and needs God?

Will you always get together with the moms from church, or will you choose to start a new meet-up group with moms you don't know?

Will you join in the church softball league, or get on a team in the community league?

Will you keep going to lunch with the same coworker, or will you break out of your comfort zone and start building a relationship with someone new?

Will you pay at the pump or take the extra couple of minutes to go inside to pay so you can start developing a relationship with the guy who works the cash register?

Will you be salt? Will you be light?

Maybe someday it could be said that there used to be no light, but now, because of you, there is no darkness.

• • •

Now What?

> Read Matthew 5:3-15.

> Where is a place you could infiltrate with the love and goodness of God, so that you can shine his light in the darkness?

> Pray that God's light would emanate from you everywhere you go. Ask him to show you how you can shine his light at your job, school, or neighborhood.

Day 4

MORE THAN ONE WAY

Pray for us, too, that God will give us many opportunities to speak
about his mysterious plan concerning Christ. That is why I am here in
chains. Pray that I will proclaim this message as clearly as I should.

COLOSSIANS 4:3-4

SOMETHING'S BEEN BOTHERING ME for quite a while. I think it's time for me to talk about it.

It's the expression, "There's more than one way to skin a cat." We've all heard it. We've all probably even said it.

What's wrong with us?

More than one way to skin a cat? First, who is skinning cats? And second, how many different ways are there? I can't imagine more than just the basic way, and I don't even want to imagine that!

I did some research. Apparently, the phrase goes back to at least the 1840s. The best evidence indicates that the debate was whether to skin a cat when it's dead or still alive. Are you kidding me?

I also learned that another old British phrase was "There are more ways of killing a cat than choking it with cream." What? And another: "There are more ways of killing a dog than choking him with pudding." What sicko tried to kill a dog with pudding?

More Than One Way

You might be wondering: If I'm supposed to talk to people about my faith, how do I do it? If I get the opportunity, what do I say?

I've got good news. It turns out there's more than one way to talk about Jesus.

The book of Acts in the Bible is the history book of the first Christians, and all through it we see them telling people about Jesus. If you read it, you'll notice that they do it in all kinds of ways. So if you think you don't know the right way to do it, well, that's not a problem, because there is no one right way to do it.

In Acts we see that instead of having a prepared speech they gave everyone, the Christians tried to meet people where they were at, then walk them toward God and faith in Jesus.

So make sure you meet people where they're at. When I was in college, I had a friend named Dan. I wanted him to know Jesus. But if I had immediately thrown it all out there and asked Dan to believe, I'm convinced it wouldn't have gone well.

So I was patient. I led with love, trying to be a good friend to Dan and looking for ways to serve him. When I had the opportunity, I would quickly mention to Dan something that happened in church or that I had read in the Bible. After months of that, I had earned trust with Dan, he was more open, and I found a good time to throw it all out there. I asked Dan to put his faith in Jesus. Pretty soon, he did.

Last year I made a new friend named Jeff. My plan was to do the same, to be patient and first develop our friendship. But immediately Jeff started telling me he was searching for something and asking me about my faith. I realized he was ready, so I threw it all out there. I asked Jeff to put his faith in Jesus. Pretty soon, he did.

Meet people where they're at. After you've led with love and earned trust and the time is right, throw it all out there. When you do, make sure what you say is intelligible.

Don't use religious language, like "That's when I was washed in the blood of the Lamb and born again."

Don't show off the Bible words you know, like "And you, too, can experience justification."

No, just talk in everyday language and try to make it as simple as you can.

You could say something as simple as, "There's a God who loves you. You may have walked away from him, but he's never stopped loving you. He sent Jesus for you. And he's inviting you to come back to him. To have a relationship with him, that will give you a better life now and life with him forever in heaven."

Or you could use a Bible verse. You don't need to memorize thirty of them. You could just use one that you write down for your friend to read or that you show him or her in your Bible. For instance, Romans 6:23: "For the wages of sin is death, but the free gift of God is eternal life through Christ Jesus our Lord."

Then you explain it: "It says *wages*. Wages are something you earn.

"It says *sin*. Sin is when we do wrong. When we make the wrong choice. When we live in a way that is not loving. When we dishonor God.

"It says *death*. Death is an ending, an unwanted separation, the end of relationship. So this verse says that what we have earned, through our sin, is death.

"Then the next word is *but*. 'But the free gift of God.' A gift is something you're given that you haven't earned. It's something someone who loves you gives you just because her or she loves you.

"God has offered you the gift of *eternal life*. What is eternal life? It's life without end, without separation. It's life where relationship, specifically with God, never ends.

"How is that possible? The next phrase says, 'through Christ Jesus our Lord.' The idea is that this is only possible because of

Jesus. When Jesus died, he took what we deserved by taking away our sin. He made it possible for God to offer us the gift of eternal life. And that gift is available to you if you just say yes."

That's not the *right* way to explain it; that's just *one* way you can explain it. The key is to keep it simple.

Another thing we see the early Christians doing in the book of Acts—and it's still very effective today—is sharing their stories. When you have the opportunity, share your story of how you came to believe and the difference it's made in your life.

The truth is there's more than one way to share your faith and present Jesus to people. And it's something you *have* to do.

There is also more than one way to skin a cat. But fortunately, that is not something you have to do.

•   •   •

Now What?

> Read Acts 17:22-31 and Acts 26:1-29.

> In these passages we see Paul sharing his faith in different ways, in different situations, and with different audiences. One approach we see Paul take is to share his personal story. Have you ever shared your "God story" with anyone? Why don't you take some time to prepare by outlining it? What was your life like before giving it to God? How did you come to faith? What has God done in your life since?

> Pray for your church. The mission of the church is to bring glory to God by making disciples out of people who are not currently believers. Pray that your church becomes increasingly effective in that mission.

Day 5

TOO IMPORTANT NOT TO SHARE

"Everyone who calls on the name of the LORD will be saved."

But how can they call on him to save them unless they believe in him?

And how can they believe in him if they have never heard about him?

And how can they hear about him unless someone tells them?

ROMANS 10:13-14

HAVE YOU EVER KEPT SOMETHING SECRET?

When my wife, Jennifer, and I were first married, I was doing an internship at a church in Louisville, Kentucky. It was a great place to live, and the people were very nice. For instance, for my internship I had to bring packages to the post office almost every day. I'd usually get the same post-office worker, and he'd ask, "What's in your package?" I would tell him, and he'd say, "Oh. Well, if it were a book, I could have given you a special rate!"

One day my wife received a chain letter from a friend. It told her to send one pair of women's underwear to a specific lady she didn't even know, and send letters to six of her friends asking them to get involved, and she would eventually get thirty-six pairs of underwear in the mail. Weird.

She went out and bought a pair of underwear, stuck it in a package, and said, "Vince, I need you to take this to the post office tomorrow and mail it, because I can't leave work to do it."

I walked into the post office the next day with a secret. I walked into the post office praying that my normal guy wouldn't be there to ask, "What you got in your package? If it's a book, I can give you a special rate."

"No, but do you have a special deal on sending women's underwear?"

Thankfully, he wasn't there that day. Because I had a secret I didn't want him to know. I didn't want anyone to know!

The Secret

In November of 1993, I proposed to my then-girlfriend. She said yes.[*]

Let's imagine Jen then exclaimed, "I can't wait to tell my parents!"

"What?" I say. "Tell your parents? I don't think we need to tell your parents."

"What do you mean?" Jen asks. "Of course we're going to tell my parents."

"No," I insist. "Listen, this is just between you and me. We don't have to go telling anyone. That's not necessary."

Jen is confused. "You don't want to tell anyone?"

I'm emphatic. "No one."

I convince her, and we don't tell anyone.

Soon we set a date for the wedding. Jen tells me, "I've picked out some great invitations! Everyone is going to be so excited."

"Whoa. Invitations?" I object. "No, Jen, we're not inviting anyone. Listen, we're going to find a minister to do this. It will be just you and me. I mean, it's *our* relationship. There's no reason to get anyone else involved."

Jen is pretty upset but finally agrees.

Trying to find something to get excited about, she says, "Well, I guess we need to go ring shopping."

---

[*] Poor girl had no idea what she was getting herself into.

"No," I respond, "I'm *not* wearing a ring."

"What do you mean?" she asks. "That's a sign of our being married. It shows people the commitment we've made to each other."

I try to assure her: "C'mon, Jen, *we'll* know that we're married. We don't have to show it off. No one else needs to know."

That's not what happened, but let's say it was. If it were true, you would wonder about my commitment to my wife. Why am I so embarrassed by her?

Too Important

Jesus says, "If anyone is ashamed of me and my message, the Son of Man will be ashamed of that person when he returns in his glory and in the glory of the Father and the holy angels."* Paul writes, "I am not ashamed of this Good News about Christ"** and "How terrible for me if I didn't preach the Good News!"***

I realize it can be difficult to talk about your faith. You might worry about not knowing the right thing to say or how to answer tough questions. You may be afraid that people will reject you. But even so, we *have to* tell people about Jesus. Why?

If we don't, what kind of commitment do we have to Jesus?

And God tells us to.

And if we don't, how will other people find out about Jesus?

There was a Mercedes-Benz ad some years ago that showed one of their luxury cars smashing into a wall during a safety test. A narrator came on and talked about a safety feature the company had developed. And then the narrator interviewed an engineer from the company. He asked why Mercedes-Benz had not enforced its patent on the technology, instead allowing other car companies to copy it.

The commercial ended with the engineer saying, "There are some things in life that are too important not to share."

---

* Luke 9:26.
** Romans 1:16.
*** 1 Corinthians 9:16.

People *have to* know about Jesus—for this life and the eternal life to come.

It's just way too important to keep it secret.

• • •

Now What?

> Read 1 Corinthians 9:16-23.

> Who in your life needs to hear the Good News about Jesus? How could you (lovingly) create an opportunity in the next week to (lovingly) tell them about God's love for them and how they can put their faith in Jesus? Do it!

> Pray that God will give you an opportunity to share your faith with someone this week. Who might that be? What relationships have you already been investing in?

DISCUSSION QUESTIONS

WEEK ONE: HUNGRY

1. When were you the hungriest you ever remember being? Why were you so hungry? What would have been the perfect food in that moment?

2. Read Mark 10:46-52.

3. What do you think Bartimaeus might have heard about Jesus that led him to call out as Jesus passed by? What did you hear about Jesus that originally led you to seek him?

4. Bartimaeus was obviously very hungry for Jesus and what Jesus could bring to his life. Has your hunger for Jesus and what he can bring to your life been increasing or decreasing lately? Why?

5. Is it possible that your other desires—for success, friendship, sex, etc.—are masking your true hunger, which is for God? How could you see this being true in your life?

6. Because he wanted Jesus and what Jesus could do for him, Bartimaeus shouted out. His shout led him to get what he desired. If you're hungry for more of God, what do you need to do to get what you desire? What practical steps could you take?

1. What is your favorite story? (Maybe it's a fairy tale or tall tale you learned as a kid? Or a book you've read or movie you've seen as an adult?) What about that story appeals to you?

2. An article called "Why We Need Stories" suggests, "Without them, the stuff that happens would float around in some glob and none of it would mean anything." Do you agree or disagree? Why?

3. Within the concept of "story" is the idea of a "metanarrative" —an overarching story that provides a narrative and meaning to everything. Do you think such a metanarrative is possible without God? If there were no metanarrative, would that mean life is meaningless?

4. Read Psalm 139:13-16.

5. In what way does Psalm 139 make God sound like an author who is giving each of our lives a story?

6. How has knowing God made sense of your life and given it meaning and purpose?

WEEK THREE: NEW

1. When were you the most excited you've ever been to get something new? What was it? A toy when you were a kid? A car? A house? An outfit?

2. Read 2 Corinthians 5:17.

3. Obviously, when people put their faith in Jesus, it's not that they literally become completely new people. They still have the same hair, fingernails, personality, and tone of voice. So what exactly do you think this Bible verse is referring to? What about the person is new? And what old is gone?

4. How have you experienced newness in Christ? In what areas of your life have you felt new since finding faith?

5. In what areas of your life do you still long to experience newness in Christ? Where do you still feel like the old you and in need of change?

6. If God wants to make you new, but there are still areas where you're feeling like the old you, what might you be doing (or not doing) to keep him from doing his work in your life?

WEEK FOUR: ABIDE

1. When have you felt closest to God? What did you do, or what happened, that led you to feel so close to him?

2. Read John 15:1-8.

3. Jesus proposes a relationship in which we abide in him. What do you think he meant by the idea that we could live inside him?

4. When you read the Bible, does it make you feel connected with God? How do you think you could read the Bible in a way that helps you feel more connected to him?

5. When you pray, does it make you feel connected with God? How do you think you could pray in a way that helps you feel more connected to him?

6. Jesus said that our hearts are drawn to whatever we give our money to. How do you think giving more money to God could help you feel more connected to him?

WEEK FIVE: COMMUNITY

1. What was the best group experience you've ever had? What made it special?

2. Read Acts 2:42-47 and 4:32-35.

3. What about this Christian community most catches your attention?

4. What aspect of this Christian community do you find most appealing?

5. What aspect of this Christian community makes you most nervous?

6. What would it take for you to go deeper into Christian community? How could you get past your fears and any facade you put up, and really experience authentic and supportive community?

WEEK SIX: OBSTACLES

1. What do you typically do when you're going through a difficult time or are down in the dumps? Does it help?

2. Read Romans 5:1-5.

3. The first two verses in this passage share some of the amazing things that happen when we put our faith in Jesus. How have you personally experienced some of the "highs" of life in Christ?

4. Verse 3 says that we can rejoice in our "problems and trials." How have you personally experienced some good coming out of times of doubt or pain?

5. When we're suffering, why is it difficult to remember that God loves us?

6. How can knowing God's love and being empowered by the Holy Spirit (who fills our hearts with his love) help us when we're struggling? Have you ever experienced that?

1. If you could ask God one question, what would it be?

2. Read Psalm 13, which was written by King David.

3. In the first verse, David complains that he feels forgotten by God. When have you felt that way? When you did, did you talk to God about it, or was it a time when you stopped praying?

4. In the next verses, David complains about the evil in the world, and that people who do evil often seem to win. What are some of the things in the world that really bother you? Do you talk to God about those things?

5. In verse 5, David's tone changes and he goes from expressing angst and anger toward God to expressing trust and hope in God. What do you think caused this shift? Do you think maybe honestly sharing his feelings with God helped David to change his perspective and attitude? How might it help you to be more open with God with your questions?

6. David wrote other psalms where he questions God. Later in the Bible, God called David "a man after my own heart" (Acts 13:22). Does it surprise you that a person who questioned God so much is someone God would hold in such high esteem? Do you think it's possible that one of the reasons God looked so favorably on David is that David came to him with all his questions?

WEEK EIGHT: MISSION

1. Who was the person who helped you to come to faith? What was it about that person, or about how he or she shared Jesus with you, that really helped you?

2. Read 1 Peter 3:15-16.

3. This passage begins with instruction to truly live our lives with Jesus as our Lord. If our goal is to help other people put their faith in Jesus, why might living lives of true love and obedience to Jesus be the best foundation?

4. We're told to always be ready to answer people's questions about our faith. How can you make sure you're prepared to answer people's questions?

5. This passage assumes that people will ask us questions about the hope we have as believers. What kinds of things might people see in the life of a Christian that would lead them to ask questions? Has that happened to you?

6. Why do you think it's so important that we talk to people about our faith with gentleness and respect?

ABOUT THE AUTHOR

VINCE ANTONUCCI pastors Verve, an innovative church that seeks to reach people who work on and live around the Las Vegas Strip. The television series *God for the Rest of Us* chronicles Vince's work there. In addition to pastoring and writing books, Vince leads mission trips around the world, speaks nationwide, and performs stand-up comedy in Las Vegas. Most of all, he loves spending time with his wife, Jennifer, and their two kids.